A IS FOR OX

is for Ox

A short history of the alphabet

Lyn Davies

THE FOLIO SOCIETY
2006

First published in Great Britain in 2004
by Ottakar's Plc

Copyright © Lyn Davies 2004, 2006

Lyn Davies has asserted his right to be identified
as the author of this work

Published by the Folio Society 2006 by arrangement
with Lyn Davies

Design and original illustrations
© Lyn Davies 2004, 2006

BINDING ILLUSTRATION
The foreground illustration is based on the letter A in
Luca Pacioli's *De Divina Proportionæ* of 1509.
The background is a detail of a Pompeian inscription,
from a rubbing made by the author

Layout, typesetting, editing, printing and binding
by Butler and Tanner Limited
Frome and London
www.butlerandtanner.com
Set in Berthold Baskerville, $9\frac{1}{2}/12\frac{3}{4}$
Printed on Voluprint Wove and bound in full blocked cloth

Second printing 2006

original concept, illustration and design   *Lyn Davies*
consultative editor   *Dr Steven Roger Fischer*
editor   *Julian Flanders*
proofreader   *Helen Burge*
index by   *Indexing Specialists (UK) Ltd*

for
Peter, Gerry, David
and Dara

LEGE FELICITER

ABCDEFGHIJKLMNO
abcdefghijklmno

Contents

Illustrations

8

9

Introduction
What is the alphabet?

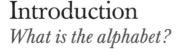

In 1998–9 newspapers around the world ran a story about two inscriptions found in the Egyptian desert. Usually newspaper editors regard 'Archaeologist finds inscription' stories about as newsworthy as 'Baker makes loaf' stories. However, this story excited interest because the inscriptions were not only thought to be the oldest alphabetic inscriptions ever found, but they might also help experts to tell once and for all where the alphabet came from.

The alphabet is such a fundamental part of our lives we very rarely stop to wonder where it came from – or why its letters are shaped the way they are, how they came to signify the sounds they do, how it all actually works. So, what is the alphabet?

The alphabet refers to the western set of letters (there are other sets) that runs, at least in English, A B C D E F G H I J K L M N O P Q R S T U V W X Y Z. The name comes from the Greek words for the first two letters – *alpha-beta*. The word *alphabetic* refers to the system in which these and other sets of signs (such as Greek and Cyrillic) are used.

An alphabetic system works by using a kit of parts, or *letters* (the speech signs in an alphabetic writing system), to make up words. The most important characteristic of these signs is that, ideally, each represents just one simple sound known in linguistics as a *phoneme*. So the word 'desk', for example, is made up of four signs, representing four separate sounds: the sound /d/ as in dog; /e/ as in pet; /s/ as in pass; and /k/ as in lark* (English is, of course, notorious for its complicated spelling, but this is to do with the language's history rather than its underlying system of writing). Arabic and Hebrew writing are both referred to as alphabetic because they use this system, even though neither uses *the* alphabet – although their letters did grow from the same roots. Alphabetic, theoretically, suggests one-sign-one-sound.

A characteristic of the alphabetic system is that the kits contain relatively few parts – they only need enough signs to represent the sounds in the language they are expressing. So 26 signs, used singly or in combination, are all that is needed to express the sounds in English speech. The Greeks need only 23, the Russians 33. The Chinese, whose system is not alphabetic but more *logographic*, roughly defined as a one-sign-one-*word* system, have over 60,000 signs to express their several languages, though most of those are now archaic or highly specialised and only 6000 are actively used.

So much for the system. Did the inscriptions found in the Egyptian desert and reported so enthusiastically in the newspaper articles tell us where the alphabet came from? That is still the subject of discussion – and is likely to be so for some time – but the discoveries are suggesting some fascinating possibilities. However, the question remains, why are letters shaped the way they are? How did they come to signify the sounds they do? And why does A stand for ox?

---

* When a *sound* is referred to throughout this book, the letter primarily associated with it is shown between slashes // as in the examples above. For a complete list of the sounds these letters-between-slashes represent, turn to page 61.

1

How did writing begin?
The Sumerians and Egyptians 4000–2000 BC

The alphabet is not the world's oldest form of writing. People were using other systems of written communication for perhaps 2000 years before the emergence of our one-sign-one-sound system. Some systems were *syllabic*, using one sign to represent combinations of sounds. Others were mainly *logographic*, using one sign to represent one word. Some systems combined both of the above with other elements. But where did all these ways of writing start? How did writing begin?

THE SUMERIANS

To the northwest of the Arabian Gulf, in what were once green lands between the lower Tigris and Euphrates rivers, lay part of the area known as the Fertile Crescent. Now dry southern Iraq, it is a land that has been settled and fought over for thousands of years. Archaeological evidence suggests the presence of large towns as long ago as the fourth millennium BC, and for this reason the area is also known as 'the cradle of civilisation'.

The builders of these towns are known as the Sumerians. It is not clear where they came from before they settled, but the archaeology

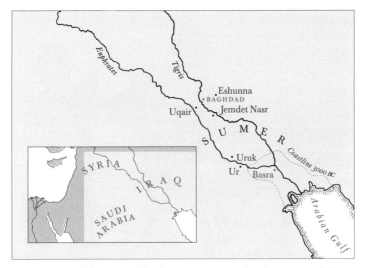

Early cities around the Tigris and Euphrates rivers, now southern Iraq, are part of what is known as 'the cradle of civilisation'. (Modern features are marked in orange.)

suggests that by the beginning of the fourth millennium BC they had acquired flourishing systems of agriculture, were using the Tigris and Euphrates to irrigate their lands, were making pottery from the abundant local clay and making bricks to build houses. They became very successful, not only producing enough food and other commodities for themselves, but also creating surpluses to trade with each other and with neighbouring towns. By 3500 BC two of their main settlements had grown into a substantial town, called Uruk (referred to as Erech in the Bible). By 3000 BC the town was a rapidly expanding city, with a population estimated to be as large as 50,000. Religion was a fundamental part of Sumerian existence, with priests forming the higher levels of their social structure, and large temples, stone-built, high on ziggurats at the heart of their cities. It is these remarkable people that are widely believed to be the inventors of writing.

Sumerians depicted on a casket decoration from the city of Ur, c. 2400 BC.

During the course of archaeological digs in areas of Sumerian settlement, large numbers of small clay objects about the size of marbles have been recovered, some dating from as early as 8000 BC. They were of various three-dimensional shapes – spheres, cones, diamonds, pyramids and so on – some plain, others marked with dots or lines. For many years, archaeologists thought they were nothing more than ornaments or items of jewellery but as more and more turned up they noticed the repetition of certain shapes. Scholars began wondering whether they were tokens used in trade, for example, one shape perhaps denoting a sheep, another a bundle of straw.

Archaeologists also began finding hollow clay objects, about the size of a child's fist, that seemed to have other objects inside them. When further research into these finds was carried out, including X-ray examinations, they were found to contain numbers of the clay tokens. Interestingly there were often markings on the outside of these envelope-like objects that appeared to correspond with the shapes of the tokens inside. If the clay tokens were trade-related, were these new finds, dated from some time in the fourth millennium BC, early receipts? Were they proofs of sale showing what had been agreed in transactions, invented to be more difficult to tamper with than a handful of loose tokens? Perhaps: but even if they were, what have they to do with writing?

Clay tokens (above) and a few of the corresponding symbols.

One theory for why writing began was that it emerged from a need such as this – to record everyday things for accounting. As society and trade became larger and more complicated so there became literally too much to remember. A means of recording transactions would have been required. Many scholars believe the tokens were a first step in this process.

For example, a Sumerian merchant holds three tokens of a particular shape which remind him that he owes a client three sheep next time he's in town. The next step, sealing the tokens in the envelope and using the corresponding symbols on the outside, perhaps came about to stop clients saying a merchant actually owed them four sheep but he'd lost one of the tokens. The next step was to realise the tokens were not needed: simply write the symbols on a clay tablet. Uruk is well known for the vast number of clay tablets recovered archaeologically, recording lists of all kinds of items such as food, livestock and building materials. This last step, though almost an exercise in common sense, would actually have been a revolutionary leap in the story of writing. Instead of one *object* (a token) representing another *object* (a sheep), a written *symbol* was being mutually agreed upon as representing the sheep.

Along with the innovation of token-represents-object, scholars believe the Sumerians developed a token-represents-number system. One token of particular shape for a certain quantity, another token of a different shape for another quantity and so on. These are also thought to have been represented as symbols on the envelopes and, later, on the clay tablets. This would have been another revolutionary leap: a *symbol* representing not an *object*, but an *idea* – the earliest examples of what are known as *ideograms*.

There are problems with this token theory however. The number of symbols that appear on the clay tablets to resemble token shapes is thought to be too small as a proportion of the total number of symbols used – 1500 by some estimates – to be a viable explanation of how writing began. And some of the symbols for certain objects appear much less frequently in the tablets than scholars might have expected: sheep, for example, were an important commodity in Sumerian trade, yet the sign thought to represent them only appears a very small number of times in all the tablets found in Uruk.

So, it is suggested that token-to-sign-to-writing, instead of being *the* way, might be just one of several ways that contributed to the emergence of writing in Sumer in the fourth millennium BC. But what do we mean by 'the emergence of writing'?

What scholars currently believe to be examples of the earliest system of writing are on the tablets already mentioned, made of clay, baked hard in the sun. Examples collected are of various shapes and sizes and are all covered in simple little pictures which were scratched into the clay while it was still wet. Each of the pictures, usually referred to as *pictograms*, are thought to record a commodity – food, grain, land and so on – and are invariably accompanied by circular or fingernail-shaped impressions representing quantities. They demonstrate the earliest systematic use of symbols to record what could otherwise only be communicated by speech, which is a fundamental aspect of the practice we think of as writing.

However, the symbols on these tablets could not be described as 'complete writing'. The symbols might be capable of listing what a person bought, but not of describing how they were feeling or what kind of day it was: in short, they were not capable of communicating what scholars refer to as 'any and all thought'. To be capable of this another revolutionary leap had to be taken, perhaps the most important in the story of writing: the *symbols* had to become representative of *sounds* rather than *objects*.

Clay tablet from Uruk, recording a sale or purchase of barley.

c. 135,000 litres

of barley

accounting period, 37 months

signature of the official responsible (Kushim)

final account (?)

barley used for exchange (?)

bee + leaf = belief   *bee + 4 = before*   *2 + bee + oar + knot + 2 + bee = to be or not to be*

Imagine a pictograph of an object, a bee for example. If the symbol ✿ only ever represented the insect the symbol would only ever have one meaning and only be capable of being part of a list. However, if the ✿ changes use to represent the sound /bee/, it can be used to mean not only the insect, but also part of a word with the sound /bee/ in it, or the word 'be'. Suddenly it becomes possible to write words whose meanings are difficult to represent with a picture: belief, before, to be or not to be. This principle, known as the *rebus* principle, was thought to have been discovered by the Sumerians around 3700 BC, probably inspired by their largely monosyllabic language. It made their symbols capable of much more than making lists: it made them capable of complete writing.

CUNEIFORM

If the rebus had not been discovered it is unlikely the Sumerians' system of writing would have developed into anything more than a means of making lists by using pictograms. However, the expansion of the system, and its ability to express not only simple commodities and quantities but almost anything expressed by speech, also assured its continuing development in appearance.

The pictograms became more simplified and abstracted. Those on tablets from the mid to late fourth millennium BC suggest the use of a pointed tool to draw them. However, by the mid-third millennium the signs were obviously being created by a different tool, one with a wedge-shaped end, and through its use the signs had become more abstracted. As the illustration shows, these new signs clearly resemble the older, pictographic signs but their formation with the wedge-ended tool created a more consistent look to the writing, now known as cuneiform.

Pictographic signs (top), 3500–3000 BC, and their cuneiform versions (below) c. 2400 BC.

By 2500 BC cuneiform had settled into a regular syllabic system of writing, that is each sign representing composite sounds, such as *pa*, *re*, *mu* and so on. This began, in the previous millennium, by one sign standing for not only the word it was originally drawn for, but other words that sounded the same. For example, say this sign $\lor$ represented *mu*, the Sumerian word for 'plant'. In Sumerian *mu* also meant 'year' and 'name' so $\lor$ would come to represent those words as well. Eventually, according to the rebus principle, $\lor$ would be used wherever the sound /mu/ occurred in Sumerian words.

Sumerian cuneiform: part of an account of crops and fields from about 2700 BC .

Cuneiform was recognised as such a successful means of writing that even the people who eventually conquered the Sumerians, the Akkadians, began using it to express their own language, and after them the Babylonians and Assyrians to express theirs. The last datable use of cuneiform occurred in the first century AD.

Say 'ancient writing' to most people and they will probably think of the complex and mysterious collections of signs on Egyptian monuments. Hieroglyphs, from the Greek *hierogluphiká* meaning 'sacred carvings', is the name given to the system of writing that was used around the Nile Delta for over three millennia. For many years scholars believed it was the world's oldest form of writing, in fact the debate still goes on in certain quarters. However, it is now generally believed that the early Egyptians gained the idea of writing through contact with the Sumerians. It is a possible explanation of one of the enduring mysteries about Egyptian hieroglyphs – where did they come from? – because there is so far no evidence of an evolution in their writing system.

The Egyptians themselves gave no historical account of how they learned writing, calling their system *medoo neter*, or 'god's words', believing that writing was a mystical gift from their god Thoth. There are rock carvings on the edges of the Sahara from around the sixth millennium BC and examples of designs used on pottery and weapons from the middle of the fourth millennium (called the *pre-dynastic* period in Egyptology), all of which may be precursors of signs used later in hieroglyphic writing. But nothing has yet been uncovered to demonstrate any

The ibis-headed Egyptian god Thoth.

stages of development before fully formed hieroglyphic writing appears. Recent excavations in Abydos, an important pre-dynastic centre of Egyptian culture 300 miles south of Cairo, have provided archaeologists with the suggestion that the Egyptians were applying the rebus principle to pictograms around 3400–3200 BC, but not where they got the idea from, leaving speculation that it came from the Sumerians. By 3100 BC the Egyptians were using a sophisticated system of writing that remained virtually unchanged for the next 3000 years.

Egyptian hieroglyphs were a collection of signs, many of which could be used in two ways. One way was to represent single words, in which case they are known as *logograms*. The other way was to represent sounds, where they are called *phonograms*. The phonograms are further grouped into those signs that represented:

    i) single sounds, *uni-consonantals*, e.g. ⌇⌇⌇⌇ stood for /n/

    ii) double sounds, *bi-consonantals*, e.g. ⌷ stood for /mn/

    iii) triple sounds, *tri-consonantals*, e.g. ♀ stood for /nkh/.

The Egyptians had two final roles for their hieroglyphs. Because many characters could be used as both logograms and phonograms, characters called *determinatives* were employed to help tell the reader which was which. For example, 𓏞 could mean the sound /sh/, but the addition of one determinative made the word *scribe* 𓏞 𓀀, and of another made the word *write* 𓏞 𓏜.

The last use for the signs was as *phonetic complements*, where they were added to a character in order to emphasise a particular pronunciation: ⌷ denotes the sound /mn/, but a scribe might add ⌇⌇⌇⌇ denoting an /n/ sound to emphasise the original character's sound ⌷ ⌇⌇⌇⌇. The name of the Pharaoh Tutankhamun, Ruler of Upper (and Lower) Egypt, in its original hieroglyphic form, demonstrates many of these uses:

-   *uni-consonantal* /t/ sound
-   *uni-consonantal* /w/ sound
-   *tri-consonantal* /nkh/ sound
-   *uni-consonantal* /i/ sound (approx.)
-   *bi-consonantal* /mn/ sound
-   *phonetic complement* /n/ sound
-   *logogram* meaning 'ruler'
-   *logogram* meaning the city 'Thebes'
-   *logogram* meaning 'Upper Egypt'

The Egyptian use of formal hieroglyphs was accompanied from around 3000 BC by an informal version written with a reed pen on papyrus called *hieratic*. Whereas the hieroglyphs were used exclusively for the sacred and ceremonial, hieratic was a more abstract, rapidly written (or *cursive*) version of the signs used for administration, business and everyday correspondence. By the seventh century BC it had developed into an even more cursive and abstract form known as *demotic*.

Among all these different uses of the hieroglyphs, those with the most significance for the story of the alphabet were the single-sound uni-consonantals. Basically the Egyptians had invented what we could call alphabetic signs, but the sacred conventions governing the uses of hieroglyphs prevented official scribes from ever using the characters by themselves in an alphabetic way. However, *informal* use of the single-sound hieroglyphs around 2000 BC may be the way our alphabet came to be born.

OTHER HIEROGLYPHS AND LOGOGRAMS

One of the fascinating aspects of the study of writing is the similarity between the early stages of writing by different peoples around the world. We associate the word hieroglyph primarily with the Egyptians, but it has come to be used for similar writing systems from other civilisations. The Hittites, living in what is now southern

Early Chinese signs from a bronze inscription, c. 1000 BC.

Part of a Hittite inscription, c. 1000 BC.

Mayan hieroglyphs from a sarcophagus inscription, c. 680 AD.

Turkey, used hieroglyphs, perhaps directly inspired by the Egyptians'. The Chinese, as far as we know, had no contact with the Egyptians, yet they too were using simple pictures as logograms, in the mid-second millennium BC, the precursors of some of the 6000 characters actively used today. The Maya of central America were writing during the first millennium AD by using hieroglyphs that, though very different in appearance from the Egyptian, were very similar in systematic use, including logograms and phonograms, with determinatives and phonetic complements. It appears that throughout the world people came to writing through the systematic use of pictograms at pretty much the same time. The beauty and mystery associated with their hieroglyphs led them to develop and guard their different traditions. However, mystery and tradition were eventually overtaken by something less romantic: efficiency.

2

The alphabet emerges
Egyptians, Canaanites and Phoenicians 2000–800 BC

The story of how the alphabet emerged from among all the established writing systems is still a matter of debate. However, many
scholars think that the system probably evolved from the use of
single-sound hieroglyphs in Egypt. And it is a matter of tradition
that the Phoenicians, seafaring traders from the Levant who spoke
a Semitic language, spread the established alphabet throughout
the Mediterranean, crucially passing it on to the Greeks. But from
the time the system emerged to the alphabet being considered
'established' is a period of almost a thousand years. What happened
in between?

FROM HIEROGLYPHIC TO ALPHABETIC WRITING, *c.* 2000 BC
Why do scholars think the alphabet grew out of the single-sound
hieroglyphs? That particular branch of hieroglyphs was the one
where each sign denoted just one consonant. Egyptians found them
particularly useful for spelling foreign names: Egyptian names
were made up of sounds that could generally be represented by the
whole range of hieroglyphs, but foreign names were made up of
sequences of sounds not found among the logographic, two- and

three-sound hieroglyphs, so they were usually spelt out, using the single-sound signs, one sign for each sound in the name (■ ▪ 𓆑 𓂝 ⌐ 𓏭 𓏌 P-t-o-l-m-e-s: Ptolemy). But there is evidence to show that these signs were also used unofficially.

Several inscriptions, thought to date from *c.* 2000–1900 BC, showing hieroglyphs used in an alphabetic way were found in an Egyptian town called Kahun. And in the 1990s, two alphabetic inscriptions were found, also thought to date from *c.* 1900 BC, at Wadi el Hol on the ancient road between the cities of Abydos and Thebes. These inscriptions, mentioned in the introduction, were on a rock face among more orthodox hieroglyphic graffiti written by Egyptian soldiers guarding the desert road. Experts believe these new inscriptions are also alphabetic, even though they have not been translated, because the hieroglyphs used are mostly of the single-sound type.

What these discoveries lead scholars to think is that, while the official scribes used hieroglyphs according to sacred practice unchanged for 3000 years, and other educated Egyptians used a slightly smaller range of hieroglyphs in an established graffiti style, there was a casual, everyday use of the single-sound signs in the simpler, alphabetic fashion. And there is the possibility that the easier-to-learn, single-sound hieroglyphs may have been used by foreign workers or soldiers to write in their own language. How and why it happened is not yet known – this is one of the crucial points in the story

Two signs from the Wadi el Hol inscriptions, thought by some scholars to be very early versions of our letters A (top) and E.

for which experts still have a frustrating lack of information – but around 2000 BC, some single-sound hieroglyphs started to be used with their sound values changed to suit the expression of *Semitic* rather than Egyptian speech.

Egypt had long had dealings with the culturally related groups known as the Semitic peoples. They lived in areas roughly corresponding to the modern countries of Lebanon and Israel, and though separated into distinct tribes and kingdoms (Canaanites, Israelites, Moabites etc.), they appear to have been closely related linguistically.

At various times between 2500 and 1200 BC Egypt had been a neighbour to be feared, taking people as slaves and bringing south-ern areas of Semitic territory under their imperial administration: but at other times they were more peaceful and traded with various communities. It is within these areas that some of the earliest examples of Semitic alphabetic writing have been found. Inscriptions on jars, shards of pottery, a dagger and javelin heads, found in settlements to the west of the Dead Sea and River Jordan, are thought to date from *c.* 1600–1400 BC. They are early illustrations of the crucial change in the alphabet's history, the use of Egyptian single-sound hieroglyphs to represent single sounds in Semitic speech – the earliest ancestors of the sounds we still ascribe to some of our letters today. How this change came about is not certain, but in this Canaanite context it may have happened through trade – a stable trading community, needing a script that was easy to learn and

Canaanite inscriptions found near Jerusalem.
TOP *potsherd from Shechem.*
MIDDLE *dagger, Lachish.*
BOTTOM *potsherd, Gezer.*

write, perhaps adopted the quick, 'unofficial' use of single-sound hieroglyphs from their Egyptian business associates. However, another explanation (that might have brought the transition about even earlier) is that it could have been invented by the group of people thought to be among the most frequent users of writing in the ancient world: slaves.

THE SPHINXES OF SINAI

In 1905, the archaeologist Sir Flinders Petrie was excavating a site near old Egyptian turquoise mines at Serabit el Khadem on the Sinai Peninsula. He found several inscriptions – on tablets, walls and little ornamental sphinxes – that did not appear to be in Egyptian and could not be translated. Unlike orthodox Egyptian writing they used a relatively small number of signs – Petrie counted around 30 altogether – which led him to think that the mysterious inscriptions could be alphabetic. If the inscriptions weren't in the Egyptian language though, what language was it? It was known that slaves from Semitic territories had been used by the Egyptians to work the mines. Could the inscriptions be in Semitic?

The Egyptologist Sir Alan Gardiner, working a decade later, suggested that a group of four signs that was often repeated in the inscriptions 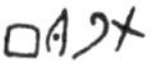, if given sound values from Semitic speech, could be translated as *b'lt*. The writers probably wrote their inscriptions using only consonants and no vowels as the Egyptians had, so Gardiner speculatively replaced them and came up with the word *Ba'alat*, which he translated as 'Mistress', the Semitic name by which the Egyptian goddess *Hathor* was known in the locality. This speculation has since become accepted as proof that the inscriptions were indeed written alphabetically in a Semitic language.

It was also Gardiner who proposed a name for each of these early Semitic signs, the first sound of which would be the sound signified by the sign. He suggested Semitic words translated from the Egyptian meanings of the hieroglyphs that looked most like the new signs.

For example, the sign ⴳ, meaning ox in Egyptian, he called *aleph*, the Semitic word meaning ox (see page 62 for an explanation of the sound signified by the letter). The sign ⊓ he thought looked like the Egyptian hieroglyph for reed hut or house, so he gave it the name *beth*, the Semitic word for house, and so on. They turned out to be virtually the same as the names of some of the letters in the modern Hebrew alphabet, which has led scholars since Gardiner to use it as a source of names for letters in other early alphabetic inscriptions (and it is the source for many of the names in the alphabet section of this book).

LEFT *One of the sphinxes and its inscriptions from Serabit el Khadem. The word* b'lt *is highlighted, and can be seen on the figure beside its left flank.*
RIGHT *The inscription from another Serabit sphinx with* b'lt *highlighted.*

So who wrote these inscriptions on the little votive offerings? Traditionally, slaves in ancient times were the most frequent users of writing, performing for their masters and mistresses nearly all their writing tasks. So was there some class of slave in this region, in the early part of the second millennium BC, using Egyptian hieroglyphs to express sounds in their own Semitic speech? Again, at an important juncture in the story there is as yet no proof, only speculation. It would seem to be an extraordinary stroke of luck to hit upon the place where the momentous change in sound values occurred, so many scholars are only content to state that these are the earliest examples of Semitic alphabetic writing found so far.

The dating of the inscriptions from the Sinai excavations has been a matter of discussion for some time, with many scholars suggesting that they are younger than the Canaanite inscriptions. However, the current consensus is that they are older, perhaps dating from around 1800–1600 BC.

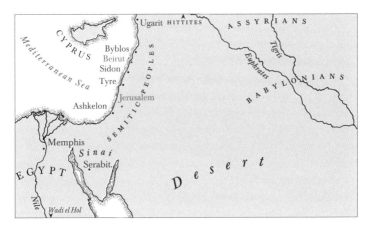

WHAT HAPPENED NEXT?

Between 1800 and 1200 BC the territory under the influence of the Semitic peoples was a melting pot of different writing systems. The southern territories tended to reflect the Egyptian influence using alphabetic writing and signs based on the hieroglyphs. Further north, near what is now Beirut, communities tended to have more contact through trade with the empires further north and east: the

Babylonians and Assyrians with their cuneiform syllabic writing, the Hittites of Anatolia (today's Turkey) with their hieroglyphic syllabic writing, and to the west the Minoans and Cypriots with their 'Linear' syllabic writing. So the writing of the northern Semitic communities reflected these influences in their own syllabic systems.

Alphabetic cuneiform from Ugarit.

Over the course of 800 years the different writing systems evolved and spread over the area. The different influences – alphabetic and hieroglyphic styles from the south and syllabic, linear, and cuneiform from the north, west and east – were mixed and developed by the different Semitic communities for varying lengths of time. For example, between 1800 and 1200 BC in the city-state of Byblos on the coast, a syllabic system of writing (showing influences from the west, east or north) used characters that were distinctly Egyptian (or southern) in character. Whereas further up the coast in Ugarit from *c.* 1500–1200 BC an alphabetic system with cuneiform-like characters was used. Efficiency was probably the deciding factor, eventually. Alphabetic systems were much easier to learn and more adaptable to different languages than the syllabic systems, whose many pairings of consonants and vowels tended to suit very few languages. As what we now call the Bronze Age turned into the Iron Age, around 1200–1050 BC, the alphabetic, one-sign-one-sound system was becoming dominant in the region and was soon to establish itself as the most important export of the greatest traders and seafarers of the new era, the Phoenicians.

THE PHOENICIANS

Between 1200 and 350 BC, on the coast at the eastern end of the Mediterranean (what is now, roughly speaking, the Lebanon), you would have found the home territories of the Phoenicians. They are thought to have been related to the Canaanites, our name for them deriving from the Greek word *Phoenikes*. This is probably a reference to the rich red and purple dyes they made which were some of the luxury goods they traded throughout the Mediterranean.

They were, in the main, a coastal people, forming settlements that grew into prosperous trading ports and cities. Byblos, Sidon, Ashkelon and Tyre were the greatest of these, each ruled by a king. They were accomplished sailors which gave them opportunities to trade and plant cities all around the Mediterranean (Carthage, the Roman Republic's nemesis, started life as a Phoenician trading post). King Solomon of the Israelites built his great temple with cedarwood bought from the King of Tyre. On the one hand they were admired as skilled engineers and gifted craftsmen. But on the other they were seen as unscrupulous profiteers and amoral schemers – we refer to a shameless and immoral woman as a 'Jezebel', the name of a Phoenician princess of Tyre. They are thought to have been the first people to circumnavigate Africa, and it has even been suggested they may have travelled as far afield as Britain in search of gold, lead and tin – a possible explanation for the presence of gold artefacts from Crete in burial sites on Salisbury Plain.

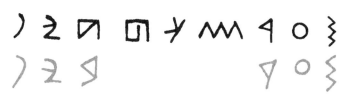

Characters from the Byblos syllabary, in use until c. 1200 BC, and below them letters from the Phoenician alphabet, used in Byblos c. 1000 BC, that may be related to them.

This adventurous, cosmopolitan people used an alphabet that appears to have developed out of a fusion of signs from several syllabic systems, including the Byblos syllabary, with the alphabetic system. The result was a regular, rather abstract collection of letters, many of which can be linked visually with the early Semitic signs, and the earliest example of which can be seen in an inscription on the sarcophagus of a Phoenician king, Ahiram of Byblos, from the eleventh century BC. The letters became the dominant pattern

Part of the inscription on the sarcophagus of King Ahiram.

throughout the region, and over the next several hundred years showed up in examples such as a calendar from Gezer from the tenth century BC and a tablet commemorating victory in battle of the Moabites over their erstwhile Israelite rulers, *c.* 850 BC. The same alphabet was passed to the Arameans, who used it to write their language Aramaic (the language spoken nearly a thousand years later by Christ) and it formed the basis of today's Hebrew alphabet. It was also passed on to the Nabateans, who were the forerunners of the Arabs, and whose alphabet is also a development of the Phoenicians'. How and when this happened is still very controversial but, most importantly for this story, the Phoenicians also passed the alphabet on to the Greeks, the next people to dominate the eastern Mediterranean.

Moabite inscription from the ninth century BC.

3
The alphabet spreads
Greeks, Etruscans and Romans 1000 BC–AD 100

How and when was the alphabet borrowed from the Phoenicians by the Greeks? There is at present too little evidence to describe categorically this pivotal point in the story. However, something that is not in any doubt is the Greeks' introduction of vowels into the alphabet – the Phoenicians, for the most part, had depended on context to tell them how to pronounce the consonants of their inscriptions. The alphabet also underwent several important changes at the hands of the Etruscans, before being adopted by the Romans whose refinements of line and proportion largely completed the development of many of the capital letters we use today.

CONTINUING A WRITTEN TRADITION?

For many years it was thought that the Greeks' first contact with writing was through the alphabet. The Greek historian Herodotus tells us in his *Histories*, that the Phoenicians 'introduced to Greece a number of accomplishments of which the most important was writing, an art until then unknown to the Greeks'. It is now thought that this introduction refers to early syllabic systems of writing (perhaps from Byblos), and that rather than Greece passing through a 'Dark Age' during which this writing was forgotten (after the destruction of the societies that developed it) some parts of the ancient Greek world continued to write, passing from the old syllabic systems to the new alphabet in a smooth transition – proving that Greek is the oldest continually written language in Europe from *c.* 1900 BC to the present day.

For much of its history, Greece has not been a single country or kingdom but a collection of loosely related city-states, islands, colonies and territories. Our earliest evidence for distinct societies, ancestors of the classical Greeks, were the Myceneans and the Minoans, whose cultures existed from *c.* 2000 to 1200 BC on the Greek mainland and the island of Crete respectively. These cultures, from whose era Homer drew inspiration for *The Iliad* and *The Odyssey*, were the ones thought to have been introduced to syllabic writing by the Phoenicians' ancestors. Examples of these were first discovered by the archaeologist Sir Arthur Evans on the island of Crete while excavating the Minoan city of Knossos in 1900. The Minoans had first used what looked like a hieroglyphic system (unrelated to the Egyptians'), followed by two pictographic scripts which seemed to be related to each other. Evans named these 'Linear' scripts, differentiating them by calling them Linear A and Linear B. He strove for many years to decipher the writing without success, believing it to be not Greek but a distinct language which he referred to as Minoan. When Linear B was eventually deciphered, largely by the work of an amateur called Michael Ventris, it revealed that the language was in fact an early version of Greek.

The Minoans succumbed, around 1200 BC, to sustained attacks by the raiders known as the 'Sea Peoples' (thought to be loose alliances of other Greek peoples), and their writing seemed to die out along with their culture. However, although examples of Linear A and B peter out after the suppression of the cultures that created them, Greek did continue to be written on an island apparently unmolested by the raiders.

Minoan Linear scripts.
ABOVE *Linear A*
(as yet undeciphered).
BELOW *Linear B:*
a list of tripod cauldrons,
wine jars and goblets.

Cyprus, near the Levantine coast, was an outpost of Minoan culture where Linear B had developed into a further branch of the system, not surprisingly referred to now as Linear C. What is also very interesting about Cyprus is that excavations have revealed a Phoenician enclave on the island, established somewhere between 1100 and 900 BC, where artefacts bearing Phoenician alphabetic inscriptions have been recovered. Could this be one of the points at which the alphabet started its journey from its Semitic home into Europe? Though still unproven, scholars are beginning to think this likely. What was believed until recently to be the earliest alphabetic inscription in Greek was actually uncovered in Athens, and was fairly confidently dated to 730 BC. Other material has since come to light that is thought to be older, however, while for various reasons experts were already questioning whether the eighth century BC was the earliest point at which the alphabet was used in Greece.

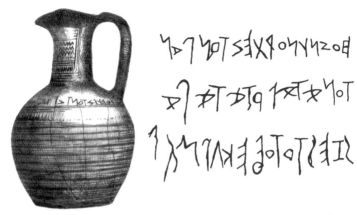

Early Greek inscription. Scratched in a continuous line around the rim of a vase and reading right to left, it says 'to him that dances so delicately'. Athens c. 730 BC

One reason stems from the direction in which Greek inscriptions were written. Whereas now we always write from left to right, for several hundred years after 730 BC the direction of Greek writing was anything but constant: some inscriptions read left to right, others right to left, while others alternated (known by the Greek word *boustrophedon*, referring to the way an ox ploughs a field). However, although the Phoenicians' inscriptions also showed all these changes in direction, by around 850 BC their direction of writing had established itself as right to left. If the Greeks had adopted the alphabet after this point, it is likely they would have also adopted the fixed direction: therefore, some scholars conclude, the Greeks must have adopted the alphabet before 850 BC.

Another curiosity is that the shapes of the Greek letters seem to resemble older versions of the Phoenician letters. Again, by *c.* 850 BC the character of letters in many Phoenician inscriptions had become flowing and cursive with long, curving downstrokes (see p. 33, the Moabite inscription), but the letters in Greek inscriptions are more upright, much less 'developed' stylistically and more reminiscent of letters from inscriptions of the tenth century BC. All this, as well as the knowledge of the close ties early on between the Phoenicians and certain Greek communities in the eastern Mediterranean, contributes to the current consensus that the Greeks had probably adopted the alphabet by the middle of the ninth century BC at the latest, and could even have adopted it as early as 1000 BC.

GREEK INNOVATION

Whenever it was that they borrowed the letters, the Greeks probably established fundamental changes in the alphabet from the beginning. The most important of these was the addition of letters representing vowels. The standard Phoenician alphabet of 22 letters represented a number of sounds that were alien to Greek speech, so they used these letters for the sounds they thought they most closely resembled in their own speech. For example, ⸙ represented a sound in Semitic speech that was not present in Greek speech (see p. 62 for an explanation of the sound), so they reassigned it to the closest sound that did occur in their speech, which was the initial /a/ sound in *alpha*. The Phoenician ⸙, called *he*, and probably pronounced like our exclamation 'hey!', stood for the /h/ sound found at the beginning of the name. But the Greeks denuded the letter of this /h/ sound and used the character for the vowel sound left over, /e/, renaming it *e-psilon*, or 'naked e', in the process.

From the point at which the alphabet was adopted by the Greeks, variations of the letterforms developed. In all the colonies, islands and other territories the shapes of the letters – though from recognisable root characters – tended to be determined by local traditions. These various styles eventually coalesced into three regional traditions. The oldest versions of the alphabet persisted in the islands of Crete, Thera and Melos. More developed versions were found in the eastern regions of Greek territory: the eastern Aegean, the area of the Greek landmass called Attica, which included Athens, and Ionia (the near coast of what is now Turkey). Finally, related styles of lettering could be found on much of the Greek mainland and the western territories including Sicily and Ischia, near Naples. This disparate state of affairs continued until *c.* 403 BC when Athens decreed that all official documents would thenceforth be written in one style, the Ionian form of the alphabet. Ionian may have been chosen because it had become a high-status script, owing to its association with Homer's *Iliad* and *Odyssey*, which were first written down in the Ionian style. However, this decree occurred after the western versions of the alphabet had become firmly established on the stage of the next scene in the story: the Italian peninsula.

THE ETRUSCANS

The Etruscans to a great extent remain a mysterious people to us, owing to a lack of record or literature about them. Their territories were situated in the north of what is now Italy, in an area roughly analogous to that of Tuscany. They were, for a short period of time around the eighth century BC, the dominant people on the peninsula, though they did not form a country or a kingdom, but instead followed the pattern of the time of establishing city-states and large settlements ruled locally, though loosely affiliated by culture and language. Their culture was in part highly original (leading some scholars to wonder whether they were native to the area at all), and partly influenced by the Greek culture, which, by that time was firmly established in the colonies in the bay of Naples, the southern coast and the island of Sicily. Their funerary rites are thought to have been the precursors of the rituals that later grew into the barbaric gladiatorial contests of Rome. However, it is by way of the funerary inscriptions, which are more or less all that is left to us to form a record of their language, that we know something of Etruscan speech and the effect it had on the alphabet.

The Greek colonists that the Etruscans came into contact with originated on the island of Euboea, east of the Greek mainland. They brought with them their version of the alphabet, containing

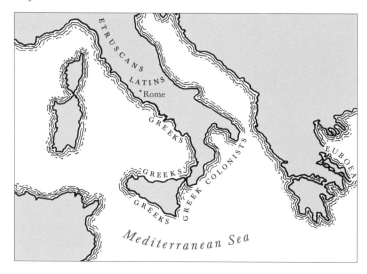

several letters which were different from those of the Ionic version that came to form the root of the present-day Greek alphabet (and one of the reasons the latter is so different from our own). For example, when the Etruscans began using the alphabet *c.* 750 BC, the letter *gamma* reached them in two forms (and ⌐. The second was the shape also used in the Ionic alphabet but, whereas it persisted in Greece to the present day (Γ), it died out in Etruscan and Roman Italy (for reasons unknown) leaving (to evolve into our letter C. The story is the same for D. The Greek *delta* came to the Etruscans in two shapes ◁ and △, the second being similar to the Ionic version that is the ancestor of today's Greek Δ. But it was the ◗ that gained dominance in Etruscan inscriptions.

The Etruscan language was very different from Greek, so several changes in the use of the alphabet occurred as a consequence. The main difference was a lack of what linguists call 'voiced stops' (see p. 66 for a little more information on these). Voiced stops are sounds like /g/ as in rag and /b/ as in lab. They are similar in sound to 'unvoiced stops' like /c/ as in rack and /p/ as in lap. So, when the Etruscans inherited from the Greeks the letter *gamma* (, which represented a /g/ sound in Greek that did not occur in Etruscan, the Etruscans used it for the closest sound that did occur in their speech which was /c/ as in rack. So the letter (that was passed on to the Romans represented not the original /g/ sound but the /c/ sound for which we still use it today. This meant that the Etruscans now had three letters representing /c/-related sounds: (, Ҡ and ⸢. So they used (in words before the vowel sound /a/, Ҡ in words before the vowel sounds /e/ and /i/, and ⸢ before /u/, as we still do today. They also dropped the use of word-names for each of the letters and referred to them by sound-names, pronounced AH, BAY, CAY (KAY), DAY, etc.

All these changes to the alphabet and its use occurred over a relatively short period of time, a century or so, and were passed on to the Romans when they began using it to write Latin *c.* 650 BC.

FINISHING TOUCHES

For many of the letters in our alphabet, the last stage of development in their shapes occurred during the course of their use by the Romans. The Roman Empire grew out of very humble origins. Initially a collection of villages and huts scattered over hills and the land between, by the end of the seventh century BC they had coalesced to form the early city of Rome. The first centuries of Rome's existence were marked by the rule of kings, ending with the reign of the Etruscan, Tarquinius Superbus, whose tyranny led to his being overthrown by the people of the city-state. The republic which was subsequently formed in 509 BC lasted until the career of Julius Cæsar threw it into crisis, his murder in 44 BC prompting a power struggle that lasted until Augustus became Rome's first Emperor in 27 BC.

By the time the villages had joined to form Rome, the people of the nascent city and its surrounding region, known as the Latini, had acquired the alphabet from their Etruscan neighbours. Inscriptions from this early period are scarce but those that remain show that the direction of writing could be left to right, right to left, or boustrophedon. By the third century BC, the direction had settled on left to right.

Part of the Lapis niger inscription, one of the oldest in Latin yet found. Late sixth century BC.

By the first century BC the Romans had developed several styles of alphabet for different purposes. Informal, quickly written letters, or *cursives*, were the everyday handwritten form of the letters, usually written on portable wax tablets with a pointed metal tool called a *stilus*. *Rustic capitals* were a stylised form of capital used for, among other things, painted notices on walls – the advertising posters of their day.

Inscriptional letters, also known as *capitalis monumentalis* and used for permanent monuments, had evolved from the rather crude shapes of the seventh and sixth centuries into more or less the shapes we use today. Apart from the proportions of the letters gradually becoming more consistent, by the first century AD single-thickness

Rustic capitals painted with a square-ended brush directly onto a wall, Pompeii.

Roman cursive.

The construction of a brush-drawn letter A suggested by the calligrapher Father Edward Catich, showing some of the strokes that evolved into serifs. Catich used the inscription at the base of Trajan's column in Rome (below), created AD 113, as his exemplar.

strokes had evolved into thick-and-thin strokes owing to the use of the flat, square-ended paintbrush, skilfully manipulated to lay out the inscriptions before cutting them into the stone with a chisel.

The other major characteristic of today's letters to grow out of the Romans' use of the brush was the serif. When the painter was laying out an inscription he would start the stroke of a letter with a short 'edging-in' stroke to ensure all the hairs of the brush were in contact with the surface of the stone: this meant that the main stroke would be a solid, smooth line of even width. And instead of ending the stroke by simply lifting the brush, it was terminated with a smooth 'edging-out stroke'. It was these strokes that evolved into the serifs.

Part of a commemorative inscription, late first century AD.

When the cutter started his work with mallet and chisel he started his cut at the point of these short strokes, making them permanent features of the letter. They not only formed attractive terminals to strokes of the letters, they accentuated the invisible lines between which the letters ran, strengthening the design of the inscription.

At the turn of the first century AD, most of the letters in our first alphabet had completed their evolution. The letter G had been invented in the fourth century BC to differentiate it from the letter C which had until then stood for both /c/ and /g/ sounds; and the letters

X and later Y and Z had been borrowed from the current Greek
alphabet specifically to write Greek words and names that had crept
into Roman vocabulary. There would be the addition of several
other letters during the course of the next 1700 years (the Romans
didn't use J, U or W), but the alphabet, some of whose letters began
life before 2000 BC, had reached the basic shapes we are familiar
with today. The only major change in use would be the addition of
the second alphabet with which we are familiar – our small letters.

4

Majuscules to minuscules

The evolution of small letters AD 100–1500

Our alphabet of small letters developed, for the most part, over a period of 1600 years. They each grew out of their capital or *majuscule* forms, gradually evolving through the calligraphic styles that were used to produce documents and manuscript books throughout the Early Middle Ages. Whereas the capital forms developed along trade routes through Near Eastern deserts and the Mediterranean Sea, the small letters emerged from the Bibles and other texts written in monastical *scriptoria* across Dark Age Europe.

BACK TO ROME

At the end of the last chapter Rome was embarking on its most glorious period but by the fifth century AD the Empire had become a vast administrative mess, that had had to be split between East and West and ruled by separate emperors in order for it to carry on functioning. The Eastern Empire was ruled from Constantinople (modern Istanbul) and was then the real power in the Imperial machine. Rome was the capital of the Western Empire in name only, having become an inconvenient place from which to rule: a sad, crumbling version of its former self. After the forced abdication of

Early Roman uncials, fourth century AD.

the last Emperor, Romulus Augustulus, *c.* AD 476, the Western Empire ceased to exist, leaving the Christian church as the only unifying force in Europe.

Before the fall of the Western Empire the Christian authorities had been producing manuscripts for ecclesiastical use throughout the Empire for nearly two centuries. A particular style of lettering had been developed for these works in order to set them apart from secular texts. *Uncials* (from *uncia*, meaning 'inch high') were a rounded, wide letterform, the earliest examples of which have been found in documents in the Coptic language from North African parts of the Empire. The characters of the letters are a consequence of the way the broad-nibbed pen used in writing them was held at a very shallow angle, in fact almost horizontally, making thick downstrokes and thin horizontal strokes. The Coptic examples are thought to have been a conscious emulation of contemporary Greek manuscripts, Greek not Latin being the main language associated with Christianity during the early centuries of the religion's development.

47

While most of the uncial shapes are recognisably derived from capital letters, some depart quite radically, suggesting that some of the shapes may have developed from other styles of writing. One style was probably the Roman *cursive*, a catch-all name given to the handwriting styles of clerks, scribes and ordinary citizens. Romans had been writing cursive forms of the capital letters since at least the first century BC. As you can see from the examples (or your own handwriting), quickly drawn letters tend to produce curves and reduce angles, so the forms of the capital letters changed when written this way. Strokes are not always tightly controlled, so lines flick above and below the main body of the letters. Shapes that became natural elements of a professional scribe's personal handwriting would have entered official documents, which were written in neater versions of the cursive style. So when later scribes were commissioned to write formal, ecclesiastical manuscripts, some of the more unusual shapes into which the capital letters had morphed (and which had become fairly commonplace) found their way into the regular uncial style.

New Roman cursive, fourth century.

Early half uncial. Roman, fifth century.

The three lines of medium-size lettering are in the insular style, from the Lindisfarne Gospels.

Another important style that was a direct development from Roman cursive was *half uncial*. This was the handwriting style of an educated person of the fourth century which gradually developed into a formal manuscript style itself. The early stage, illustrated opposite, looks like a tidied up Roman cursive, with the longer, spidery strokes above and below the lines now fairly regular upstrokes and downstrokes, or *ascenders* and *descenders* as they have come to be called.

Manuscripts were produced all over the former Western Empire in places of learning such as Benevento and Ravenna; Tours and Paris; Aachen and Reichenau; Iona, Lindisfarne and Kells. The uncial and half uncial styles were the forms of lettering used in all of these centres, but as travel became more dangerous (without local Roman administration to keep the roads safe) and communication between these ecclesiastical centres more difficult, the letterforms they produced became more and more individual, gradually changing into distinct regional styles. Places like Lindisfarne in seventh-century England and Kells in eighth-century Ireland (where Celtic Christian traditions persisted) produced manuscripts of dazzling

49

beauty and complexity such as the *Lindisfarne Gospels* and the *Book of Kells*. Among the fabulous beasts and patterns within their pages was a Hiberno-Saxon calligraphy that had developed so far from the original half uncial style that it is distinguished by the name *insular*, meaning 'from the islands'.

This disparate state of affairs continued until a change in the political structure of Europe took place in the year 789. Charlemagne, King of the Franks (or German Franconians as they are also known) issued his *Admonitio Generalis*, a document ordering educational and administrative reforms throughout what was later to become known as the Holy Roman Empire.

THE CAROLINGIAN RENAISSANCE

The undertaking for which Charlemagne (Charles the Great) is justly famous is the encouragement of learning that has become known as the Carolingian Renaissance. Though he learned to speak Latin and a little Greek, Charlemagne never completely finished learning to read and write (he said that his hand had been trained to hold a sword too long to be able to successfully hold a pen). However, he had the utmost respect for men of learning and invited the most important scholars in Europe to attend his court. Perhaps the greatest of these, Alcuin of York, was an English monk and scholar whom Charlemagne had met several times through Alcuin's diplomatic missions for monasteries in England. The Emperor invited Alcuin to his court in Aachen to take charge of the Palace school, but Alcuin also undertook the work of re-establishing the administrative network between monasteries throughout the Carolingian Empire and allied kingdoms. This included his overseeing a wholesale reorganisation of the Church's texts, which had over the centuries become a confusion of badly copied manuscripts.

New texts began to be produced and for these Alcuin supervised the use of a single letterform to replace the multitude that had evolved from the old Roman uncials and half uncials. The new

INCIPIT LIBER
EXODVS

ΛΕC SUNT
NOMINΛ
FILIORÜ
ISRΛHEL,
QUIINGRES
SI SUNTIN
ΛEGYPTÜ
CUMIΛCOB
SINGULI
CUMDOMI
BUS SUIS
INTROIE
RUNT

Ruben. symeon. leui. luda. issachar. zabulo
etbeniamin. danetnepthalim. gad etaser
Erant igitur omnes animae eorum quae egres
sae sunt de femore iacob. septuaginta quinque
Ioseph autem. inaegypto erat Quomortuo et
uniuersis fratrib: eius omniq: cognatione sua.
filiisrl creuerunt. et quasi germinantes mult

The Grandval Bible, a fine example of the Carolingian system of using minuscule for the main text, uncial for introductory passages and Roman capitals for titles.

style was a recognisably 'small' letterform rather than a stylised capital, hence the name, *minuscule.* Carolingian minuscule, as it has become known, was not a new letterform but an adaptation of forms that had been used in central Europe for 50 years or so and had developed mainly out of the half uncial form.

In Alcuin's scriptoria the minuscules were refined and used as the main text letterform, along with a clarified version of uncial for introductory passages. Pages were laid out according to a specially designed grid (just like the grids used by book designers today) that not only rationalised the positions of text but harmonised letter sizes. Titling passages were written in a Roman capital, a pen-drawn version of the inscriptional letterform from the turn of the first century, consciously drawing a connection between the old Empire and the new. Subsequent innovations included the use of uncials at the beginning of sentences (the first systematic use of capital letters with small letters) and regular word spaces, both of which are still features of our writing and printing today.

Carolingian minuscule (detail from Grandval Bible).

With the return of the rule of law, travel and communication between monasteries became easier and more frequent, and the new texts in their clear letterforms began spreading throughout Europe. The old, badly copied versions of manuscripts in the great libraries began to be replaced with manuscripts displaying the new, higher standards of scholarship. These manuscripts encompassed the ecclesiastical texts of the day such as the Gospels and other books from the Bible, religious commentaries and liturgical rules. Other texts such as those in the classical canon, like Aristotle, Suetonius and Cicero, also appeared in the new script. In fact, if it hadn't been for the Carolingian Renaissance, many of these authors' works may not have survived. And while calligraphic styles gradually evolved into the dense letterforms such as the *gothics* and *texturas* of the later Middle Ages, the manuscripts inspired by Alcuin and Charlemagne's Renaissance would remain in Europe's libraries for six hundred years, waiting to inspire another.

LETTERA HUMANISTICA

The Italian Renaissance of the fifteenth century was above all an enthusiastic revival of all things classical. Themes from Greek mythology inspired painters, patterns from Roman buildings inspired architects, the Greek form inspired sculptors and classical texts inspired scholars, sending them on expeditions around Europe looking for copies of Cicero's rhetoric, Virgil's poetry and all the other works associated with the names in the classical canon. Francesco Petrarch (1304–1374) was one of the first enthusiastic bibliophiles, with a particular interest in the Roman historian Livy. Petrarch was a poet, scholar, antiquarian and thinker, all characteristics of those who came to be known during the Renaissance as *Humanists*. He also had an interest in a certain style of lettering. His handwriting reflected a careful attempt to emulate the style of calligraphy in many of the manuscripts in his collection, those in Carolingian minuscule.

He was not alone. Later Humanists followed his lead and searched out classical texts in the Carolingian letterform specifically, singing its praises in their correspondence and rejecting the contemporary styles of calligraphy (cramped northern European gothics and fat Italian *rotundas*) as ugly, practically illegible in small sizes, but above all not classical. It has been suggested that these enthusiasts may even have thought that their Carolingian manuscripts were actually Roman: they called the letterform *lettera antica* (ancient letters) after all. This is, however, a suggestion that remains unproven.

'Rotunda' lettering was the contemporary style in Italy while the Humanists were searching out the Carolingian minuscule manuscripts.

Whatever they may or may not have known about the actual age of the manuscripts, the humanist scholars had a fine eye for the detail of the letterform and many were skilled enough to emulate and even improve upon the style. Poggio Bracciolini (1380–1459) was perhaps the most important of these practitioners and is attributed with inventing a new letterform, derived from his own copying of manuscripts in the Carolingian style. During his lifetime this came to be known as *lettera humanistica*, but we now call it *humanist minuscule.* Poggio's innovations included capital letters inspired by the Roman majuscules, but written with the same pen as the small letters so that they were a more harmonious size.

Poggio's letterforms were admired by the growing band of book collectors, whose ranks were continually swelling not only with new scholars but also wealthy patrons of the arts and established

An early example of Poggio's lettera humanistica.

publishers, such as Cosimo de' Medici and Federigo, duke of Urbino. They remained, however, a select band. Many books were still being written in the old rotunda style in the commercial scriptoria of the day. These were the days before printing and only the rich could afford newly handwritten books. Publishers at that time were employers of calligraphers, the larger ones such as Vespasiano da Bisticci in Florence using 45 scribes to deliver 200 volumes to Cosimo de' Medici in 22 months. Vespasiano was one of the publishers who began using the new humanist minuscule – and one of the reasons it began to gain a wider popularity. Ironically it was also the practice that destroyed the business of people like Vespasiano and eventually assured the new letterform's immortality. Revolution arrived in the spring of 1464 when two Germans, Conrad Sweynheym and Arnold Pannartz, brought the first printing press to Italy.

THE NEW ROMANS

Sweynheym and Pannartz had travelled from Mainz in Germany where, 15 years earlier, Johannes Gutenberg had devised the system of producing *movable type* that was about to revolutionise learning in Europe. Essentially the printing was done with lots of little pieces of metal (the movable type) with a raised letter on each. These were set to form words in a line, which along with other lines were set into a block, then locked in position face up on a flat bed. The block of type was inked up and a piece of paper pressed over it then carefully peeled away to reveal a reproduction of the words in the block. The actual process of printing the page did not take much longer than it does to read the description. The publishing possibilities must have seemed limitless to the practitioners of the new art. Sweynheym and Pannartz came to Italy armed with a fount of type based on the humanist minuscule that was becoming popular, and used it to print the first book ever printed in Italy, the *de Oratore* of Cicero. The original Humanists thought the style of lettering rather crude and continued collecting and ordering their handwritten books.

o ut ín oratore optímus quíſq; eſt:ſíc ín oꝛone firmíſſ
q; ſít p̄mum:dum illud tamē ín utroq; teneatur ut ea
:ellunt ſeruētur etíá ad poꝛandum ſi quę erūt medíoc

elquale chiamano Apyron & credono
uita. Queſti ſono fiori di pꞃimauera.

¹elquale chiamano Apyron & credono
²uita. Queſti ſono fiori di primauera.

BERNARDVS BEMBVS PATER.
Ego uero fili nuſpiam eſſe libentius ſoleo;

BERNARDVS BEMBVS PATER.
Ego uero fili nuspiam esse libentius soleo;

TOP *Sweynheym and Pannartz's first roman type.*

MIDDLE *Printing by Nicolas Jenson c. 1476 followed by the same lines set in twentieth-century fonts inspired by his type: Centaur (1) and Adobe Jenson (2).*

BOTTOM *Printing by Aldus Manutius followed by the same lines set in another twentieth-century font, Monotype Bembo.*

But many people were attracted to the new style of book not because of the letterform but because it was relatively cheap. The opportunity was now there for those people who were neither particularly wealthy nor bibliographically obsessed to own books.

    Other businessmen were quick to see the possibilities and were eager to improve on the style of type. Frenchman Nicolas Jenson set up a press in Venice and in 1470 printed another text of Cicero's in what is still one of the most beautiful types ever produced (and the inspiration for several twentieth-century typefaces like *Centaur* and *Adobe Jenson*). The humanist minuscule as a printed typeform was becoming known simply as *roman* – still the term used today – and was becoming more and more sophisticated as the skill of designing (or *punch-cutting* as the process is called) was becoming better understood.

Nicolas Jenson eventually returned to rotundas and gothics to inspire his type designs, and it was another printer, Aldus Manutius, and his punch-cutter, Francesco Griffo, who eventually guaranteed the immortality of the roman letterform. Griffo obviously recognised the clarity and beauty of the humanist minuscule, but whereas Jenson had tried to describe the calligraphic qualities of the form in his type, Griffo seems to have designed types to be forms in their own right rather than attempts to emulate pen-made shapes. Manutius' business acumen ensured that the books printed with these types sold extremely well. When Renaissance Italy became the inspiration for much of the rest of Europe (remember how many plays by Shakespeare were set in Verona?) Manutius' books, and others that used types inspired by them, were affordable badges of the new fashion. Their pages of open, clear type signalled a break with the past, symbolised by the dense gothic styles of the medieval period, and ensured a future of printing and reading in a roman form of the alphabet.

ABCDEFGHIJKLMNOPQRSTUVWXYZ
abcdefghijklmnopqrstuvwxyz

*

Key eras

8000 BC–AD 1500

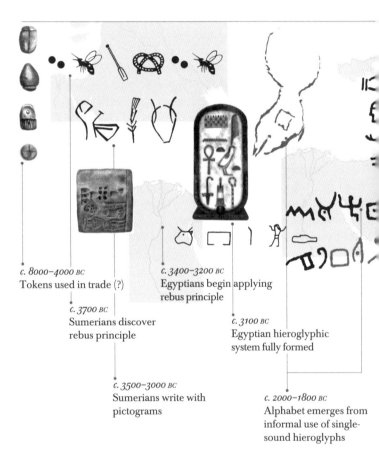

c. 8000–4000 BC
Tokens used in trade (?)

c. 3700 BC
Sumerians discover
rebus principle

c. 3500–3000 BC
Sumerians write with
pictograms

c. 3400–3200 BC
Egyptians begin applying
rebus principle

c. 3100 BC
Egyptian hieroglyphic
system fully formed

c. 2000–1800 BC
Alphabet emerges from
informal use of single-
sound hieroglyphs

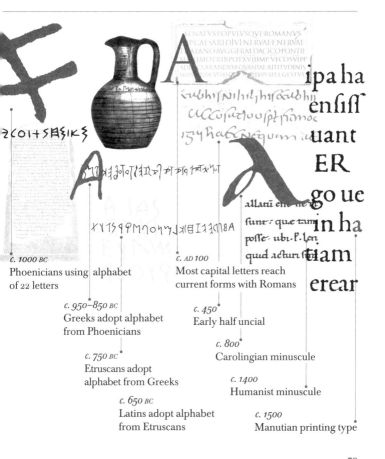

ipa ha
enſiſſ
uant
ER
go ue
in ha
tiam
erear

c. 1000 BC
Phoenicians using alphabet
of 22 letters

c. 950–850 BC
Greeks adopt alphabet
from Phoenicians

c. 750 BC
Etruscans adopt
alphabet from Greeks

c. 650 BC
Latins adopt alphabet
from Etruscans

c. AD 100
Most capital letters reach
current forms with Romans

c. 450
Early half uncial

c. 800
Carolingian minuscule

c. 1400
Humanist minuscule

c. 1500
Manutian printing type

59

The alphabet

How the letters were formed

The next pages are devoted to a letter-by-letter account of how the shapes in our alphabet developed, from pictograms to small letters. Some of the letters' shapes can be confidently traced back to Egyptian hieroglyphs formed before 2000 BC. Others appear in Phoenician inscriptions with, as yet, no clear connection to any pictographic root. Some are very recent additions to our current set of letters, not being fully established until the 1800s.

The intention is to demonstrate visually how the letters' shapes probably evolved, but nothing is certain, so the numbered captions are just general guides to times and places (in some cases very general), rather than detailed references to specific inscriptions and manuscripts.

The names given to the letters, and the words associated with them, are among the many controversial areas in the alphabet's history. The names and words used here are currently thought by some, but not all, experts to be the Phoenician names and words. Many of these come from the Hebrew alphabet, a cousin of our own set of letters, and one which still makes use of names that may stretch all the way back to their early Semitic forebears. Where the argument about the name can be accompanied with enough visual information to be of interest, the controversial names and pictograms have been included. In other places, a question mark has simply been placed after the name.

The story of the alphabet's letterforms is also the story of its sounds. To this end a few technical expressions have been included from the sciences of phonetics and linguistics. The only thing that may need a little explanation here is the use of backslashes // around letters. Linguists use these to show sounds: the letters within them usually follow a well-established pattern of phonetic signs. However, there are a few digressions here from scientific use to avoid confusion for the general reader. The signs and sounds work as follows: /a/ suggests the short sound heard in the word 'lap'; try saying the sound by itself, and do the same for /b/ as in bat,

/c/ as in cap	/d/ as in dog	/e/ as in bet
/f/ as in fan	/g/ as in goat	/h/ as in hat
/i/ as in lip	/j/ as in jam	/k/ as in kit
/l/ as in loaf	/m/ as in map	/n/ as in not
/o/ as in rot	/p/ as in pig	/q/*
/r/ as in red	/s/ as in sip	/t/ as in tip
/u/ as in cup	/v/ as in vale	/w/ as in warm
/x/ as in flex	/y/ as in yawn	/z/ as in zest

Any other pronunciations have been given their own examples at the appropriate points in the descriptions.

* /q/ has not been used: /kw/ stands in to describe the sound, as in 'quite'.

A is for ox

aleph (Phoenician) alpha (Greek)

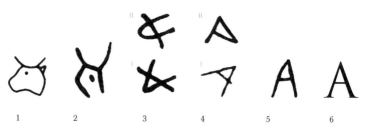

1   2   3   4   5   6

The letter **A** began life not as a vowel but as what might be described as a soft consonant. Try saying 'oh-oh' and you will get an approximation of the original sound in the sudden stop in the middle, marked here by the apostrophe: o'oh. It is this sound, which is still found in Middle Eastern speech, for which the early users of the alphabet adopted the character they called *aleph* (meaning ox) ⊲, and which developed into the abstract form ⤬ with the Phoenicians.

The Greeks adopted the character for the nearest equivalent sound in their language, a true vowel very similar to our modern 'ah'. They also took the name, (though it didn't mean ox, or anything else, in their language), but adjusted it to *alpha* to suit their pronunciation. It is the Greeks who are attributed with turning the letter from its left- or right-pointing form into the vertical form. For several centuries

7   8   9   10   11   12

two variations were used: Λ was one, but the other, 'Ionic' version, A, was the form that eventually came to be used by the Etruscans and Romans.

While the capital letterform arguably reached its most refined state with the Romans, it also began developing in several different directions again: rustic Λ, cursive ʃ, and uncial λ . These were all products of different uses of writing, carried out with different tools on different surfaces. They all contributed to the letter's development into its small letterform fixed by the Carolingians λ. Both forms were revived by the humanist calligraphers in the early fifteenth century: a was a direct emulation of the Carolingian minuscule but *a* found its place in the new cursive humanist or *italic* hand. Both *a* and a were used by early Italian printers.

B is for house

beth (Phoenician) beta(Greek)

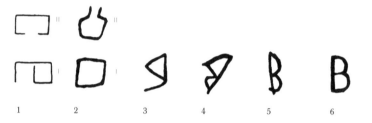

1   2   3   4   5   6

Scholars believe that the originators of the alphabet used the Egyptian 'reed hut' hieroglyph ⌐⊔ to represent the sound at the beginning of their word for house – *beth* (found in the name Bethlehem meaning 'house of bread'). The shape of the characters in Early Semitic inscriptions *c.* 1700 BC differ markedly ◻, 〇 but they are thought to come from the same root. The form of the Phoenician character 700 years later shows a more cursive version of the hieroglyph's shape ⅁.

When the Greeks adopted the alphabet, the letter's name became *beta* and acquired a lower bowl ⱽ, perhaps to distinguish it from the contemporary form of the R ᐦ. This was the shape adopted by the Romans B (the Etruscans had no /b/ sound in their language), who over the next several hundred years changed the letter's proportions to those we still see today B.

1. Egyptian
   I & II 20th cent. BC
2. Early Semitic
   I & II 18th cent.
3. Phoenician 11th cent.
4. Greek 8–7th cent.
   Athens
5. Etruscan 7th cent.
6. Roman 2nd cent.
7. Roman 1st cent. AD
8. cursive, Roman
   1st cent.
9. uncial, English
   8th cent.
10. minuscule, Carolingian
    9th cent.
11. minuscule, humanist
    15th cent.
12. printing type, Italian
    late 15th cent.

7   8   9   10   11   12

Having gained a lower bowl with the Greeks, it began to lose its upper bowl when written in Roman cursive ⁊, so beginning the development toward the form of its small letter b.

The pronunciation of letters' names in English – 'bee', for example – is unusual. Romance languages (Latin-based, like French, Italian, Spanish) call their letter 'bay', which leads scholars to think the Romans might have pronounced it in a similar fashion. Geoffrey Chaucer, in the fourteenth century, would have pronounced it 'bay' too, but not long after his lifetime a change in vowel sounds began in England (no one knows for sure why) resulting in, among other changes, 'bay' becoming 'bee'.

C is for throwing-stick

gimel (Phoenician) gamma (Greek)

1	2	3	4	5	6

What a throwing-stick was exactly, apart from a stick used for throwing, is not clear, but the Egyptians used the shape for one of their hieroglyphs. The Early Semitic character ⌐, later called *gamma* ⌐ by the Greeks, is thought to have represented a hard /g/ sound, as in the word 'gap'. This is known in phonetics as a 'voiced stop'. Its 'un-voiced' counterpart is signified by the letter C in 'cap'. Try un-voicing the /g/ by whispering: repeat 'gap' and 'cap' a few times and hear how little difference there is between the first sounds.

The change in sound from /g/ to /c/ came about through the Etruscans who did not use voiced stops in their speech (the letter B fell out of use for the same reason). So they used the (for the nearest equivalent sound in their speech, which was /c/. They probably used K and Q for much the same sound, though they used the

7   8   9   10   11   12

different characters to express different nuances in pronunciation.

The shape of the letter was not fixed immediately, and in Etruscan inscriptions different forms crop up ⌐ (as they did in Greek inscriptions, but the curved form was the shape passed on to the Romans c. 600 BC.

The Romans kept the /c/ sound for the third letter of their alphabet, and favoured it over the K and Q which they only retained for a small number of specific circumstances.

The Romans only ever used C for the hard /c/ sound: its soft /s/ sound, as in 'face' for example, came about later through a gradual deterioration of the hard version's pronunciation in certain words, through /ch/ and /sh/ to /s/. It eventually entered English speech through the influence of Norman French.

D is for door or fish

dalet (Phoenician) delta (Greek)

1   2   3   4   5   6

The origin of the letter D is obscure. Some scholars think a character showing a door ⊟ is the likeliest root, while others think one showing a fish ⌐⊳ makes more visual sense of what comes later. Both characters are found in Early Semitic inscriptions, *c.* 1700 BC. By the time the Phoenicians were using the alphabet the character thought to represent a /d/ sound was a very simple shape ◁, giving very few clues as to its origin.

The Greeks' version of the letter, which they named *delta*, developed in two directions: △, which is the capital letter still used in Greek today, and ⟨. The latter shape was adopted by the Etruscans ⟨ who, though they didn't use the letter in their own inscriptions (/d/ is another voiced stop), retained it in their alphabet long

7   8   9   10   11   12

enough to pass it on to the Romans. The Romans' letter became more gracefully proportioned, giving us the fully rounded D we still use today.

The letter's straight backstroke became reduced in size in cursive writing and the curve became more elongated with the speed of the hand 〈 . This led to the disappearance of the straight element altogether, it being easier and quicker simply to form a small loop leading into a long sweeping stroke, which is the shape found later in uncial forms 〈 . Later letters had more upright strokes and smaller bowls, which preceded the straight-backed character chosen for Carolingian minuscules d and copied by the humanist calligraphers d .

E is for hey!

he (Phoenician) epsilon (Greek)

| 1 | 2 | 3 | 4 | 5 | 6 |

The earliest forms of the letter E probably expressed the sound /h/, the name of the letter perhaps meaning and sounding like our modern exclamation 'hey!' The shape is thought to have derived from an Egyptian hieroglyph of a figure with its arms raised 𓀠. Similar characters are found in the earliest alphabetic inscriptions *c.* 1700 BC Ψ. During the next 700 years the shape became more abstract, and the character used in Phoenician inscriptions begins to look something like our modern letter ⅁.

The Greeks needed vowels where the Phoenicians had not, so took the consonantal characters closest to the sound they needed and changed their sound values. It was the Greeks that stripped the letter of its initial /h/ sound and began using the character ⅄ for an /e/ sound, renaming it *epsilon* which means 'naked e'.

1 Egyptian 20th cent. BC
2 Early Semitic 18th cent.
3 Phoenician 10th cent.
4 Greek 8th cent.
5 Etruscan 7th cent.
6 Roman 1st cent. AD

7 cursive, Roman
   1st cent.
8 uncial, English
   5–6th cent.
9 uncial, English
   8th cent.

10 minuscule, Carolingian
    9th cent.
11 minuscule, humanist
    15th cent.
12 printing type, Italian
    late 15th cent.

7   8   9   10   11   12

The Etruscans inherited the Greek letter which they found useful not only for the original vowel sound (as in 'prey'), but also for the shorter sounding vowel, as in the word 'bet' ⅃. When the Romans inherited this multi-purpose E, around 600 BC, it still had a short tail and was written pointing left or right. By the third century the letter had lost its tail and its direction had been fixed at left to right.

Again it was the quick, flowing strokes of handwritten Roman cursives that started the changes culminating in the small letterform. First of all the straight back and its right-angled top and bottom strokes became a single curve ↄ, a form exaggerated by uncials ℇ until the back stroke met the middle stroke ℮. This was the shape adopted by the Carolingians ℮, and copied by the humanist scribes in the fifteenth century ℮.

F is for peg

waw (Phoenician) digamma (Greek)

| 1 | 2 | 3 | 4 | 5 | 6 |

The sixth letter of the Semitic alphabet was a simple picture thought to represent a peg Υ now known as *waw*. It was the antecedent of five of the letters in our modern alphabet, F, U, V, W and Y, but its original use for the Semitic writers was probably to represent their /w/ sound.

The Greeks adopted this letter from the Phoenicians but adjusted its shape by bending the head Ϝ (to the left or right, depending on the direction of writing) perhaps to distinguish it from the same character used later on in the alphabet as a vowel. The new shape gave rise to a new name. As it looked like a *gamma* with two heads, it became known as *digamma*. It eventually fell out of use in Greece due to the gradual disappearance of the /w/ sound from their speech.

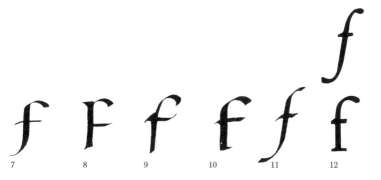

7   8   9   10   11   12

The character did survive long enough to be passed to the Etruscans who needed a letter to show their /f/ sound. They started expressing it with a combination ꟼ𐌇, but later dropped the F character in favour of 𐌚 (thought to come from the 𐌇). However, this development happened *after* the combination was passed on to the Romans, who instead dropped the 𐌇, leaving the ꟼ to represent /f/ by itself.

As with all the other letters, the capital F found its final stage of stylistic development with the Romans, its direction settled upon right-pointing, with two perfectly horizontal bars F.

Its progression to small letterform via cursives is similar to that of E, with the top bar and the backstroke fusing into a smooth curve – angles tending to become curves in cursive writing *ƒ* .

G is for throwing stick (2)

gimel (Phoenician) *gamma (Greek)*

1   2   3   4   5   6

The shape of **G** was probably an invention of the Romans. There was no letter representing the /g/ sound in the alphabet they inherited from the Etruscans, so to begin with they probably used ⟨ for both /c/ and /g/, eventually distinguishing one from the other by the addition of a spur on the letter being used for /g/ Ϲ.

    G's progression to **g**, the original shape established for the small letter, was a little less straightforward than for some of the previous letters. Its forms in Roman cursive were various: *Ϭ* , *5* (*c.* AD 100–300) showing a couple of the moves away from the formal capital and the bending of the shape into something resembling the numeral 5. This shape was formalised in uncial and half uncial

1 early Semitic 18th cent. BC	7 cursives, Roman 1st cent.	10 minuscule, Carolingian 9th cent.
2 Phoenician 9th cent.		11 minuscule, humanist 15th cent.
3 Greek 8th cent.	8 uncial, Italian 8th cent.	
4 Etruscan 7th cent.		12 printing type, Italian late 15th cent.
5 Roman 2nd cent.	9 uncial, English 8th cent.	
6 Roman 1st cent. AD		

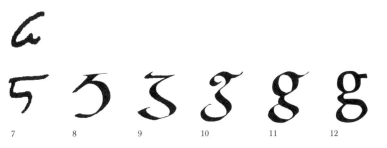

7   8   9   10   11   12

letterforms in two separate strokes of the pen: a short bar across the top and a sinuous, curving stroke leading down from it ꙅ, *c. 500*. (This is the form of the letter, used by the scribes in Irish monasteries, that didn't really die out in Ireland until very recently, in fact you can still see old road signs that use its typographical equivalent). As the letterform developed, the scribes elaborated the top bar with a curl down to the left, almost meeting the crook of the lower stroke's curve and forming an embryonic top bowl ꙅ (minuscule *c.* 800). Humanist calligraphy emulated this shape in varying degrees of looseness ꙅ : ɡ grew out of the cursive form of the hand giving us g.

H is for fence

het (Phoenician) heta (Greek)

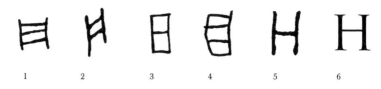

| 1 | 2 | 3 | 4 | 5 | 6 |

Historically the letter H is thought to have had a much more robust sound than it does today. The character the Phoenicians called *het* 目 (meaning fence) probably started with a heavy, back-of-the-throat sound akin to the /ch/ at the end of the Scottish word 'loch'. The cleaner sound of our modern /h/ was used in Semitic languages but already had a character assigned to it (the letter E started life as *he*).

Het changed with the Greeks: the letter they inherited from the Phoenicians Ħ expressed a sound that didn't occur in their speech, so they used it for the closest equivalent sound /h/, and renamed it *heta* (pronounced 'hayta'). The letter eventually lost the /h/ and became *eta*, used to represent another vowel.

1 Phoenician 11th cent. BC
2 Phoenician 9th cent.
3 Greek 8–7th cent.
4 Etruscan 7th cent.
5 Roman 2nd cent.
6 Roman 1st cent. AD

7 cursive, Roman 1st cent.
8 uncial, English 8th cent.
9 uncial, English 8th cent.

10 minuscule, Carolingian 9th cent.
11 minuscule, humanist 15th cent.
12 printing type, Italian late 15th cent.

7   8   9   10   11   12

The letter kept its /h/ sound long enough to be used by the Etruscans. Its shape had changed very little from the Phoenicians' form and didn't change at all until the Romans adopted it around 600 BC. Called *ha* by its new owners, it lost its top and bottom rungs leaving the form we use today H.

The small letter emerged from several hundred years of Roman cursives formed more or less as it is now, the first change being a shortened upright stroke on the right followed by the middle and right strokes fusing into a curved stroke 𝒽. This shape was given more formality by scribes for uncials ƀ, and minuscules ƀ, and copied for the humanist minuscule h.

I is for hand-and-forearm

yod (Phoenician) iota (Greek)

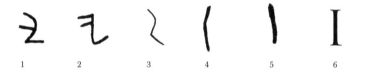

1   2   3   4   5   6

The letter I's earliest ancestor is thought to have represented the /y/ sound in Semitic speech. Its rather strange shape ꝫ may have developed from a pictograph of a hand and forearm ⌐.

The Greeks found the letter more useful as a vowel, renaming it *iota*, pronounced 'eeota', thus preserving some of the /y/ sound in the initial vowel combination. The shape began to change too: the short stroke was dropped ⟨, but it may be that the result was too like the *sigma*, later on in the Greek alphabet (ſ), so the shape was simplified even further by straightening out the angles, leaving the single stroke that has since remained unchanged (.

Now simplified in shape, the Romans complicated matters again by using it as a vowel and a consonant. Both uses are illustrated in the

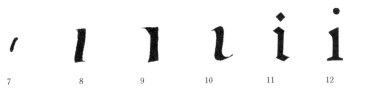

7   8   9   10   11   12

name we now pronounce 'Julius'. The Romans spelt it IVLIVS and pronounced it 'yoo-lee-oos'.

The I shrank to become the alphabet's smallest letter over several generations of Roman cursive writing, but it took a while longer to gain its dot. For several hundred years the letter was virtually hidden between Ms, Ns and Us which in calligraphy were made of strokes which looked very similar **minum** . Around the eleventh century some scribes began using a fine diagonal stroke to distinguish the i *i* (the stroke became a dot in later medieval calligraphy i). Others began replacing the letter altogether with a y, and although this affected spelling well into the eighteenth century, i was eventually re-established by clear, well spaced printing.

J is for hand-and-forearm (2)

yod (Phoenician) iota (Greek)

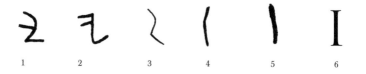

1   2   3   4   5   6

The letter J is a medieval invention that wasn't universally accepted until the eighteenth century. It was really just an extended I, used to distinguish between the original letter's two uses – as consonantal /y/ sound and vowelish /i/ and /ee/ sounds – the **J** being used for the consonant.

As we saw in I's description, this distinction in sound went back to Roman times and was demonstrated in names like IVLIVS and TRAIANVS (pronounced 'Tra-yanus' then, 'Trajan' today). So where did our modern /j/ sound come from, as used in 'John' and 'jam'? In different parts of the former Roman Empire the /y/ sound began to change as the pronunciation of Latin became more localised and concentrated (in what is now Spain, France and Italy etc.). For example, in the area that became Spain, the /y/ evolved

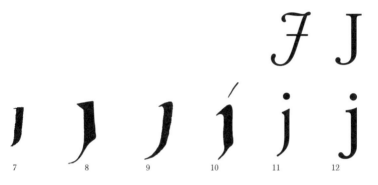

7   8   9   10   11   12

into a /h/ sound, whereas in France it became /j/. This sound was introduced into English after the Norman Conquest through newly-introduced French words ('jolly', 'juice') and in the changed pronunciation of many Latin words ('junior', 'jubilation').

For some time several forms of the small letter existed but **ı** or **ȷ** were not always used in the Y/I way described above. Sometimes the tailed version was used only at the end of words or only at the beginning, sometimes it was used exclusively. This non-standardised situation persisted in England throughout the first several hundred years of printing (1450–1700). The I was still being used by die-hards, especially where a capital J is now used, for some time into the nineteenth century.

K is for palm of the hand

kaph (Phoenician) *kappa (Greek)*

1　　　　2　　　　　3　　　　　4　　　　　5　　　　　6

The letter K is another that scholars are fairly certain originated with an Egyptian hieroglyph ⬭. The palm of the hand pictograph makes appearances in Early Semitic inscriptions Ⱳ and is thought to be the precursor of the Phoenician character ⱱ.

Examples from 900 BC show a sign that had rotated slightly and developed a long stroke ⅄; early Greek inscriptions show a *kappa* that is much closer to our modern shape ⱪ.

This is the letter adopted by the Etruscans and used, as described in the letter C, for a /k/ sound that was subtly different from what was reproduced with the letters C and Q. Though all three versions of the sound were retained with letters in the Romans' alphabet, C was used the most frequently. Q was used exclusively with their U letter for /kw/ sounds, and K was almost left out altogether, used

7   8   9   10   11   12

only for a handful of foreign names like '*Karthago*', the Roman name for Carthage.

This restricted use meant minimal development in its small form: it didn't appear very often in Roman cursives or in later, ecclesiastical texts, which were written in Latin. It only came back into its own in Middle English: the Anglo-Saxons, like the Romans, only used C for a hard /c/ sound, and didn't need a K. But when Norman French introduced the C's soft /s/ sound before certain vowels (e, i and y), confusion arose in pronunciation. So the K came to be used as a substitute. Old English words like '*cyning*' came to be spelt 'king', and the K was introduced in other words to fortify the hard /c/ sound as in 'neck' and 'flick'.

* As Roman Ks are rather rare, this is a designer's impression of how a K might have looked in the Trajan inscription on p. 43.

L is for cattle-prod

lamed (Phoenician) lambda (Greek)

1	2	3	4	5	6

A character believed to be ancestor of the letter L appears frequently in the Early Semitic inscriptions �, probably emulating the shape of an ancient cattle-prod or 'ox goad'. In some inscriptions it makes up part of a phrase, ⟩, which scholars believe can be transcribed as l b'lt, or *Al Ba'alat,* thought to mean 'the Mistress' or 'the Lady' – a Semitic name for a goddess of the Sinai region. Similar characters are found in Phoenician inscriptions *c.* 1000 BC ⟨.

However, Greek inscriptions show a letter that has become pointed ⟍ – virtually the same shape found later in Etruscan inscriptions ⟍.

1 Early Semitic 18th cent. BC
2 Phoenician 11th cent.
3 Phoenician 9th cent.
4 Greek 8th cent.
5 Etruscan 7th cent.
6 Roman 3rd cent.

7 Roman 1st cent. AD
8 uncial, Italian
   6th cent.
9 insular 8th cent.
10 minuscule, Carolingian
   9th cent.

11 minuscule, humanist
   15th cent.
12 printing type, Italian
   late 15th cent.

7   8   9   10   11   12

This shape survived for several hundred years in Roman writing but eventually the bottom stroke dropped down to the baseline .

The bottom stroke gradually shrank through the various different styles of writing: in some examples of rustic writing it is a short, heavy stroke ⌊, while in cursives it can appear as just a flick ⌊. In later uncials the separate stroke has turned into curling extension of the main stroke ૮, a characteristic adopted and refined in the Carolingian minuscule ⌊.

M is for water

mem (Phoenician) mu (Greek)

1 2 3 4 5 6

The letter M is one of the letters that still closely resembles its earliest incarnation. The Egyptian hieroglyph ᗯᗯ showing waves in water has clearly been adopted in the Early Semitic inscriptions from *c.* 1700 BC ᗯ. A virtually identical, vertical form was still being used by the Phoenicians *c.* 1000 BC ⟨. By the ninth century BC, the character shows a more stylised form ᒣ, echoed in the earliest appearances of the letter, named *mu*, in Greek inscriptions around 750 BC M. The story then is of the right stroke shortening M and the left stroke lengthening M and the middle point touching the

7   8   9   10   11   12

baseline, or not, as local tradition dictated. The form of today's letter was more or less fixed with the Romans by the third century BC.

    The main feature of the small letter's development is the smoothing of the points into curves, seen initially in Roman cursive writing ～ but more elegantly described in uncials ꟽ. Uncials from a later date show that the scribes started writing the character with a downstroke, from the bottom of which sprang the curves m. This is a characteristic emulated by the Carolingians' m and completing the development of the character still used today.

N is for snake or fish

nun (Phoenician) nu (Greek)

1   2   3   4   5   6

N is one of the letters whose name and history are not entirely agreed upon. Many experts believe the Phoenicians referred to the letter as *nun*, thought to mean 'fish'. But the consensus for how the shape developed is that it came from a pictograph of a snake, adopted from Egyptian hieroglyphs ⤙. There is currently no definite explanation for how this paradox may have occurred.

The character appears several times in Sinai in the Early Semitic inscriptions of the eighteenth century BC ⟍ and is thought to be the precursor of Phoenician characters *c.* 700 years later ꞡ , and of the more stylised shape from the ninth century BC ƴ.

The early Greek *nu*, despite its long leg remaining, is recognisably N-ish Ν, as is the Etruscan version from approximately a hundred years later Ν. Although earlier Roman versions still listed slightly

7   8   9   10   11   12

N, it was under the Latin influence that the shape we use today for our capital letter became fixed N.

What isn't straightforward is the progression from capital to small letterform. Something very close to the modern shape does appear in Roman cursives ๓ , but its evolution from the capital is not clear: ～ – ∿ – ๓ is a possible progression. Whereas the curved ฅ shape was quickly accepted as a standard shape in uncials, our current small letterform n took longer, the more capital-like ᴎ still being the preferred shape in many manuscripts as late as the ninth century. However, ๩ was the character adopted by the Carolingians (possibly because it was quicker to write, or perhaps for its neat pairing with the ๓) and later copied by the humanist scribes ๩.

O is for eye

ayin (Phoenician)   omicron (Greek)

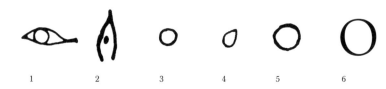

The letter **O** is another letter scholars believe can be identified with an Egyptian hieroglyph but whose use since then has changed considerably. Like *aleph*, it probably represented another consonant, but a rougher more guttural sound that doesn't appear in our speech (and so is difficult to replicate).

Examples of what is currently thought to be the letter's earliest shape, from the Early Semitic inscriptions of the eighteenth century BC, show a pictograph of an eye ⟨|⟩, clearly related to the Egyptian eye hieroglyph.

Between the eighteenth and eleventh centuries BC, the shape changed from its slim form to something rounder **O**, though the memory of the pupil was retained in some Phoenician examples which used a dot in the centre.

7   8   9   10   11   12

The rough guttural sound of the original letter wasn't present in Greek speech, so the letter was redesignated for another vowel – /o/. To start with, the letter did the job of both short and long /o/ sounds (distinctly different in Greek, like British English 'load' or 'lord'), but later on the Greeks invented a new letter to do the job of the long /o/, leaving the original letter to show the short sound. They called the original letter *o-micron* (little o) *O* and the new one *o-mega* (big o), marking the difference by simply opening up the lower part of the *o-micron* shape Ω .

The alphabet was adopted by the Etruscans before the invention of *omega*, so the O passed on to the Romans who used it for both the long and short sounds.

P is for mouth

pe (Phoenician) pi (Greek)

1   2   3   4   5   6

The Phoenician character 〉 of *c.* 1000 BC is thought to be an early ancestor of our letter P. Later forms from inscriptions of the ninth century BC are more angular 〗 and by its appearance in early Greek inscriptions it had gained a short downward stroke ⌐. The Greeks called the character *pi* (pronounced 'pee') and passed this form on to the Etruscans, who basically left it as it was except for giving the top stroke more of a curve into the short downstroke ⌐.

This shape and the Greek shape developed in different ways, with the left leg of the Greek version growing over time to be the same length as the right, giving the familiar shape still used in Greece

7   8   9   10   11   12

today Π. The Roman shape, though it appears to have remained more or less unchanged for about 300 years Γ, by the second century BC had the short right stroke curving into the main stem Ρ; and the P on the Trajan inscription, from the second century AD – though a form we recognise today – retains a trace of its origins in the fact that its curl still doesn't quite meet the main stem P.

Although the shape of the letter has remained the same in its small form, its position in relation to other letters changed through cursive writing. Its long downstroke slipped below the baseline, leading to the letter's bowl sitting on the baseline, where it remains today.

Q is for monkey?

qoph (Phoenician) qoppa(Greek)

1   2   3   4   5   6

The letter Q's history is not as complete as other letters', probably owing to its more specialised and less frequent use. Characters that scholars think are early examples appear in Phoenician inscriptions Φ, but as there are no examples from earlier periods that demonstrate a definite pictographic root (if indeed it had one), they are not sure of the letter's ultimate origin.

The fact that it has survived at all is interesting seeing that there was already a /k/ sound represented by *kaph*. The composite /kw/ sound of today's letter didn't develop until later so it seems that the sound represented by *qoph*, perhaps pronounced more from the back of the throat, was still sufficiently different in sound from *kaph* to merit its survival as a separate character.

The Greeks adopted the letter but called it *qoppa* Q, and even

7   8   9   10   11   12

though it survived long enough to be passed on to the Etruscans, it fell out of use (possibly owing to the lack of difference in sound between it and *kappa*) before the Athenean decree of *c.* 402 BC standardised the Greek alphabet.

The Etruscans, though, may have appreciated the difference in sound enough to need the letter Ϙ. It survived in their alphabet and was passed on to the Romans, who used it for all words containing a /kw/ sound, where it was accompanied by U (or V as it appeared in their inscriptions). The tail, which had shrunk over the years, was swung to the right Q and eventually grew into a flourish Q.

In cursive writing the bowl became smaller and the tail longer ↖ leading to the stroke becoming vertical ꟼ. The shape was adopted in uncials as q and copied into minuscules as q.

R is for head

resh (Phoenician) rho (Greek)

1   2   3   4   5   6

The letter R appears to have a clear lineage back to an Egyptian hieroglyph of a head ☺. Its stylised form appears several times in the Early Semitic inscriptions ☺. *Resh*, thought to mean head, was the Phoenician name for their letter ☺ leading scholars to link it with the earlier pictographic characters.

Greek inscriptions of the eighth century BC show virtually the same character ☺, but later examples show a rounded bowl and a short tail ☺. Etruscan inscriptions have examples of the earlier form, but by the third century BC Roman inscriptions also have letters with a tail that doesn't quite reach the baseline, leading to what is more or less the letter's current form R by the second century.

7   8   9   10   11   12

By the first century AD the speed of Roman cursive writing had already straightened out the bowl and leg into a single stroke and to such an extent that it is only by context that the letter is recognisable as an R ⅂. Uncials from the sixth century give the letter a new form that is reminiscent of its capital shape. The curve of the right stroke in this character preserves a hint of the angle between the bowl and the leg, and still reaches almost to the baseline ⲅ. By the time the letter was adopted by the Carolingians the stroke had drifted up almost to the horizontal, but the kink was retained ſ – a shape closely emulated by the humanist scribes of the fifteenth century r, and copied in turn by the early printers r.

S is for tooth?

shin (Phoenician)   sigma (Greek)

| 1 | 2 | 3 | 4 | 5 | 6 |

The letter S is another for which there is no satisfactory connection between its possible name and what is thought to be its pictographic form. The Phoenicians had several /s/-related sounds (known as sibilants) represented in their alphabet. Ⅰ, Ψ, ‡ are all thought to have been used for /z/-, /ts/- or /s/-like sounds, but the character currently believed to be the ancestor of our modern S was ᗯ. This is a shape that occurs in Early Semitic inscriptions, and appears to be related to the earliest Phoenician characters from *c.* 1000 BC Ⱳ.

Two characters appear to have been used by the Greeks for /s/, ⟨ and ⟩, both known as *sigma.* Both were adopted by the Etruscans, but their use depended on where and when in their territories they were being inscribed. The ⟩ form was used by the Romans whose

1 Early Semitic 18th cent. BC
2 Phoenician 11th cent.
3 Phoenician 10th cent.
4 Greek 8–7th cent.
5 Etruscan 7th cent.
6 Roman 2nd cent.
7 Roman AD 113
8 cursives, Roman 1st cent.
9 uncial, English 8th cent.
10 minuscule, Carolingian 9th cent.
11 minuscule, humanist 15th cent.
12 printing type, Italian late 15th cent.

7   8   9   10   11   12

changes amounted to a smoothing of the shape into ſ , then S.

The small letter evolved into two different characters. One simply became smaller ſ. The other, through cursive writing, developed an angle in the bottom stroke ✓ then the direction of writing changed so that the character would have been started with a straight downstroke. This was the basis of the elegant f-like form that was used as the main s character in Carolingian and many later Medieval manuscripts ſ. However, it gradually became relegated to an alternative form of S, being used only where /s/ sounds appeared at the beginning of words. This convention continued to be practised in printing, surviving as late as the eighteenth century.

T is for mark or brand

taw (Phoenician) tau (Greek)

1   2   3   4   5   6

The shape of the letter T has changed very little over the alphabet's history. Its simple form is thought to have been a branding mark and occurs several times in the Early Semitic inscriptions ✝, ✗ etc., and in Phoenician inscriptions of the eleventh century BC ✗ and later.

The form found in most Greek inscriptions is 𝖳, the top element having been lost from the middle stroke, and is the shape passed on to the Etruscans and Romans 𝖳.

This form remained fairly stable even through the speed of Roman

7   8   9   10   11   12

cursive writing ⲅ, but a flick at the end of the downstroke Τ, led to the whole stroke beginning to curve slightly. This in turn led to the curve becoming the main feature of the letter ⲧ.

This was the shape used in the Carolingian exemplar ⲧ, but unusually was not the letter copied by the humanist scribes of the fifteenth century. The shape they preferred, and the one that survives today, has more in common with the calligraphy of the thirteenth century ⲧ than that of the ninth.

U is for peg (2)

waw (Phoenician) upsilon (Greek)

1   2   3   4   5   6

The shape of the letter U is relatively new, compared with much of the rest of the alphabet. However, it is one of the characters that grew from the original root character *waw* Y.

When the Greeks adopted their letters from the Phoenicians, they used an adjusted *waw* shape for their sixth character Ϝ but they added an unchanged *waw* for use as a vowel, calling it *u-psilon*, probably pronounced with pursed lips and high tongue like the French word *tu*.

This shape Υ was passed to the Etruscans who used it for the closest equivalent sounds in their speech which are thought to have been /oo/ as in 'spoon' and /u/ as in 'bus'. In early Etruscan inscriptions the shape remains a distinctive Y-ish shape whose formation is clearly one long stroke with a shorter one added. However, as time went on the long leg shortened and the short leg lengthened, eventually forming a V, the shape passed on to the Romans.

7   8   9   10   11   12

They not only used it for the vowel sounds /oo/ and /u/, but also a consonant, /w/, both forms seen in the names IVLIVS ('yoo-lee-oos') and VALERIVS ('wal-air-ee-oos').

The development of its small letterform began to occur in rustic, and cursive ∨ writing. Its uncial shape ⱴ became accepted as the small form of V, the older, pointed form being preferred as the capital letter, though the shapes did become interchangeable over the next several hundred years.

In fifteenth-century calligraphy a convention arose (that eventually passed into printing) wherein v was written for /v/ and /u/ occurring at the beginning of words, and u was written wherever else /u/ and /v/ were used (for examples in printing see V). It was only in the eighteenth century that the current convention of u for /u/ and v for /v/ gained general acceptance.

V is for peg (3)

waw (Phoenician) victorie (Norman French)

The letter V's formation as a shape has already been covered in U: the important point is that the shape existed before the current sound. The /v/ didn't appear in Latin-based speech until the tenth century. As with the /c/ sound changing to /s/ and the /y/ changing to /j/, so /w/, in different parts of the Roman Empire, began mutating.

Its first stage of change was from /w/ to /b/. The Latin word *taverna* was pronounced 'ta-wair-na' by the Romans. A slackening of the lips and mouth in the pronunciation produces a sound that starts sounding like 'taberna', which is what it became in most of the post-Empire territories. From there the sound mutated again from /b/ to /v/, so that the word *taverne* in Norman French acquired a /v/ sound in the middle, surviving in English as 'tavern'. Old English already had a /v/ sound, but had used F to show it until the Norman scribes

1 Phoenician 11th cent. BC	7 rustic, Roman	10 minuscule, Carolingian
2 Phoenician 9th cent.	1st cent.	9th cent.
3 Greek 8–7th cent.	8 cursive, Roman	11 minuscule, humanist
4 Etruscan 7th cent.	1st cent.	15th cent.
5 Roman 3rd cent.	9 uncial, English	12 printing type, Italian
6 Roman AD 113	8th cent.	late 15th cent.

7   8   9   10   11   12

began modifying and consolidating English spelling. They used the small letterform $\mathcal{U}$ to express a /v/ as well as the /u/. This situation persisted throughout stylistic developments in calligraphy uirgine (*uirgine*, i.e. virgine, *c.* 1450).

The later convention that put v at the beginning of words and u elsewhere saw vpon (upon), haue (have) and euer (ever) in seventeenth-century English printing. But even in the later 1400s in Italy and France, printers were beginning to use v only for /v/ and u only for /u/: in French and Italian speech /v/ appeared at the beginning of words more often than /u/ so the previous convention created an association between v shape and /v/ sound, leaving the rest to u. However, this convention didn't become generally accepted everywhere else until the late eighteenth century.

W is for peg (4)

waw (Phoenician)   *wynne (Old English)*

1   2   3   4   5   6

The fourth letter to trace its history back to the Semitic *waw* character is W. Two Us together began appearing as a way of expressing the /w/ sound in Germanic languages around the ninth century AD. It was one way among several at that time in Europe – u+i and u+a were others – but the double-U was a method that became prominent during the Carolingian Renaissance.

The Normans, in their consolidation of English and French writing, used uu, as in Edwardus, replacing the Anglo-Saxon practice of using a rune ƿ called *wynne* to represent /w/. Its eleventh-century capital version comprised two V shapes and its name reflects its

7   8   9   10   11   12

antiquity: double-U harks back to the time when the V was inter-changeable with the U shape and sound. In continental France the shape took longer to gain acceptance, reflected in the French name for the character: *doublevé* was named after the V shape was fixed to the /v/ sound and U to /u/.

By the fourteenth century the two Us had become a single letter 𝕾 (English *c.* 1400). Printing later reflected these shapes, but the double letterforms persisted, even though cut as a single piece of type vv ,VV. By the eighteenth century, however, true double-Us had become widely accepted W.

X is for ?

samekh (Phoenician) ksi (Greek)

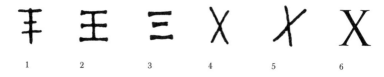

1   2   3   4   5   6

The letter **X** can be traced back to one of the four Phoenician sibilants (/s/-related sounds). Early examples date from *c.* 1000 BC ╪.

It was a letter used by the Greeks to express /ks/ sounds that occurred in their speech. Its early form had lost the little bottom tail but by the fifth century BC, the middle stroke had been lost altogether Ξ.

The people of eastern Greece used different versions of the alphabet to those of western Greece, and it was the western Greeks that passed on their letters to the Etruscans. Their version of the alphabet used Χ instead of Ξ to express /ks/, and it is this version

1 Phoenician 11th cent. BC	7 cursive, Roman	10 minuscule, Carolingian
2 Greek, Ionic 6th cent.	1st cent.	9th cent.
3 Greek, Ionic 5th cent.	8 uncial, English	11 minuscule, humanist
4 Greek, Achaean 7th cent.	8th cent.	15th cent.
5 Etruscan 7th cent.	9 uncial, English	12 printing type, Italian
6 Roman AD 113	8th cent.	late 15th cent.

| 7 | 8 | 9 | 10 | 11 | 12 |

that crops up in early Etruscan inscriptions Χ. Whereas in Greek the sound had occurred at the beginning, in the middle and at the end of words, it appears that the Etruscans only used it in the middle and at the end of words, leading scholars to think that they would have, like us, called the letter 'eks', rather than 'ksi' like the Greeks.

It is generally thought that the Romans originally had no need of a character expressing /ks/ or /eks/, so the letter did not appear in Latin inscriptions (apart from its use in numbering). However, by the first century BC they began using the character specifically to spell Greek names.

Y is for peg (5)

waw (Phoenician) upsilon (Greek)

| 1 | 2 | 3 | 4 | 5 | 6 |

The letter Y is the last of the *waw*-derived letters: but its Greek name shows it was also called *upsilon*, like U. How can the same Greek letter be in the alphabet twice?

The history of U described how the Etruscans picked up a letter from the Greeks that had a distinctive shape Y. This changed over time, passing on to the Romans, *c.* 600 BC, as a V which was used for /oo/ and /u/ (as in French *tu*) sounds. In the meantime, the Greek letter remained virtually unchanged, except for the refinements of proportion which led to Y.

During the course of 700 years Roman society adopted many aspects of Greek culture, a fact reflected in their vocabulary, which included many Greek words and names. However, they lacked letters to express some of the words' sounds accurately, so around

7   8   9   10   11   12

the second century AD, they adopted two Greek letters, including *upsilon* again.

It was the clear difference in sound between the Greek Y and the Roman I and U that caused the letter's adoption, but by the fourth century AD, this difference was becoming less apparent. Y was starting to be used in situations hitherto covered by I, especially for consonantal sounds.

Its use by the Norman scribes after 1066 led to the dying out of another rune-derived character called *yogh*. Y's use as a more visually distinguishable letter for /i/ led to its almost substituting the letter altogether. Although printing re-established the i in many spellings, the y was left in others, notably at the end of many words, for example Henri becoming Henry.

Z is for ?

zayin (Phoenician) zeta (Greek)

1   2   3   4   5

The /z/ sound in Semitic languages of the second millennium BC, is thought to have been represented by I. It was established in seventh place in the Phoenician alphabet appearing in inscriptions from the eleventh to ninth centuries as ⟋ and ⟋.

The letter was adopted by the Greeks to express the similar /dz/ sound in their speech and named *zeta* ⏋, developing over time into the shape we recognise today.

The Romans had no /z/-like sound in their speech, so had no need of the letter, until loan words from Greek like *zodiacus* led them to adopt the character in order to spell them.

---

* As Roman Zs are rather rare, this is a designer's impression of how a Z might have looked in the Trajan inscription on p. 43.

1 Phoenician 11th cent. BC
2 Phoenician 10th cent.
3 Phoenician 9th cent.
4 Greek 8th cent.
5 Greek 1st cent. AD
6 insular 8th cent.

7 minuscule, Carolingian
 9th cent.
8 cursive, English
 14th cent.
9 minuscule, humanist
 15th cent.

10 cursive, humanist
 15th cent.
11 printing type, Italian
 late 15th cent.

6   7   8   9   10   11

When the Romans did pick up the letter they also picked up the name, *zeta*. *Zeta* and *upsilon* were the only letters in the Roman alphabet to have names that were not simple sounds, similar to our own *ay bee cee dee*... etc. The Normans introduced their eleventh-century French derivations of *zeta* – namely *zéde* and *zé* – into English, both surviving long enough to be taken to America with the Pilgrim Fathers. But whereas in the States *zee* became the preferred name, probably to be more in keeping with the sound of other letters' names, *zed* survived as the letter's name in England and much of the Commonwealth.

The alphabet's development   *c. 2100 BC–AD 113*

Egyptian	Early Semitic		Phoenician	
		aleph		aleph
		beth		beth
		gimel		gimel
		daleth		daleth
		he		he
		waw		waw
		het		het
		yod		yod
		kaph		kaph
		lamed		lamed
		mem		mem
		nun		nun
		ayin		ayin
				pe
				qoph
		resh		resh
		shin		shin
		taw		taw
				waw
				samekh
				waw
				zayin

Greek		Etruscan	Roman
⊅	alpha	Ⱥ	A
⅌	beta	Ᏸ	B
⅂	gamma	⟨	C
△	delta	▷	D
⅃	epsilon	⅀	E
⟨	digamma	⟨	F
			G
⊟	heta	⊟	H
⟨	iota	∣	I
⼅	kappa	Ⱪ	K
⌋	lambda	⌊	L
Ⲙ	mu	⋈	M
⅄	nu	⋈	N
ơ	o-micron	○	O
⅂	pi	⎱	P
Ⳇ	qoppa	⎰	Q
◁	rho	⎰	R
⟨	sigma	⟨	S
⏉	tau	⏉	T
⼂	u-psilon	⋁	V
Ⅲ ⅹ	ksi	ⅹ	X
Υ	u-psilon		Y
⅂	zeta		Z

5

The alphabet now

New hieroglyphs, visual languages and text messaging

The alphabet has been incredibly successful in colonising the world's means of communication. Even in countries that hitherto have been bastions of logographic writing, such as China and Japan, the Latin alphabet is spreading, due to its ease of learning, its association with western culture and its being the primary script in use on the Internet. However, alphabets are not the all-conquering systems they at first appear to be, and in certain areas of communication they lose out to systems of writing that one might have assumed dead and buried.

HIGH-SPEED COMMUNICATION

Nowadays, hieroglyphs are associated with ancient cultures, high priests, and imposing stone monuments. So people are surprised to find that they encounter hieroglyphs every day, in fact they are an essential supplement to our alphabet-based, day-to-day communication. For example, road signs are basically hieroglyphs. They may not be the sacred carvings of the word's original meaning (although some people might argue otherwise, when we think of the car's exalted position in today's society), but they do work in much the same way that many ancient hieroglyphs did. Signs can be

logograms or ideograms. Their essential quality, making them better than alphabetic-based communication for use as road signs, is the rapidity with which their meanings can be understood. Imagine how distracting it would be to have to read warning signs written out in full: even at slower speeds
'Danger, slippery road surface ahead' would be too much to take in at a glance, especially if it was not well placed, as many road signs are not. Drivers would probably catch the word 'danger' before passing, consequently leaving them nervous and confused as to the warning. However, the ideographic version of this message manages to communicate all this information at a glance. It works in a similar way to the Egyptian hieroglyphic system: the red triangle hieroglyph gives the basic message – danger – while the addition of another hieroglyph, acting rather like the determinatives described on page 21, modifies the meaning of the red triangle, informing drivers of the specific danger to be encountered.

This message is also more or less international. You do not need to know the *word* for the object in the sign to understand its *meaning*. Many concepts can be described in pictures – which are not language-dependent – making them intelligible to almost anyone, whatever their language. Alphabet-based communication *is* mostly language-dependent, so a sign saying 'no smoking' is not intelligible to someone who does not speak English, as *défense de fumer* isn't to those without a knowledge of French.
But the sign above right could be read by anyone familiar with the *concepts* of smoking and of something crossed being forbidden.

The principles illustrated above have led some scholars to believe that it may be possible to create a language based on signs that would be universal, understood by people whatever their language.

It is an attractive concept, but how likely is it? Work was carried out in the mid-1970s by the United States Department of Transport and the American Institute of Graphic Arts to design a set of signs for use in public places such as airports, for people in a hurry and/or who didn't speak English. Many of the resulting signs are still in use around the world today, but the design committee drew attention to difficulties in the project – and problems that would be encountered by anyone trying to create a 'visual language'. They concluded that the effectiveness of any system was limited to services that could be represented by an object. They recommended that the signs should still be used in conjunction with alphabetic-based messages. Complete writing will always require a 'phonographic element' – some representation of sound – and therefore will always be predominantly language-based. The dream of a universal writing system with a shared script will only come true when everyone begins to speak the same language.

So will our alphabet remain unchanged for the foreseeable future? Undoubtedly: road signs and visual messages in airports are useful supplements to alphabetic communication but we are hardly likely to use them when we write to each other. However, the ways in which we use the alphabet may change: look at the way text messaging has given rise to different ways of writing. Apart from the common txt msg practice of dropping vowels from words and letting context indicate meaning – taking the use of the alphabet back to pre-Greek days *c.* 1100 BC – we also have the use of single letters as phonograms, commonly U for *you*, C for *see* and so on. Characters such as numbers, already in use as ideograms, are used according to the rebus principle for other similar-sounding words: 2 for *to* and *too*, 4 for *for*; or they can be used syllabically in words like 2NITE, B4, L8R etc. Obviously none of these uses is entirely new – many have been common in graffiti for years – but their use together, along with the picture messages available with mobile phones, amount to an intriguing new system of pidgin writing, with words coming not from different languages but being made up from different writing systems.

Texting may amount to nothing more than a fashion that will pass in a short time, but it is interesting to observe the processes that form it. These processes have cropped up again and again in the development of writing systems: the constant innovation to find more efficient means of expression; the experimentation in form associated with the tools being used to write; wanting to be part of a particular tribe or social group, so using the means of expression associated with it. The system forms and builds by new people learning what has gone before and trying out their own ideas. It is not the creation of a single mind but the result of exchange between many.

Perhaps this allows us to catch a glimpse of the earliest stages of the alphabet's development. If we can readily understand how easy it is for modern texters to pick up a system and find ways to improve it, we can perhaps also imagine someone from the Semitic lands leaving a simple message for a friend. The friend, delighted with the idea of using Egyptian hieroglyphs to express their own language, writes something back. Other people are shown the idea and more minds are inspired to add signs until there are enough for a complete system of expression, which is taken up by yet more people who develop and improve it and pass it on to others.

We are, unfortunately, left with only fragments of this early story – an offering to a goddess, a name on a dagger, graffiti scratched on a limestone cliff in the desert. But some of the gaps in our understanding can perhaps be filled by the realisation that today we are driven by the same impulses that have driven people throughout history – the impulse to express ourselves and record that expression, to list what we own, to write our names in order to give them some permanence – and that it was these very impulses that led, around four thousand years ago, to the birth of the alphabet.

Bibliography

This is a full list of the sources used to write and illustrate *A is for Ox*, but I would like to highlight several of the books in order to express my gratitude to their authors and to provide some ideas for further reading.

My own introduction to the subjects of writing and the alphabet came through reading *A History of Lettering* by Nicolete Gray and *The Story of Writing* by Donald Jackson: sadly, both are currently out of print but second-hand copies are worth seeking out. *Alphabet* by David Sacks also looks at the alphabet letter by letter, and *The Story of Writing* by Andrew Robinson is a well-illustrated survey of many different writing systems. *A History of Writing* by Steven Roger Fischer gives a more detailed account of all aspects of writing.

Anderson, Donald M., *The Art of Written Forms* (Holt, Rinehart and Winston, Inc., 1969).

Baines, P., Haslam, A., *Type and Typography* (Lawrence King Publishing, 2002).

Boardem, Griffin and Mary, eds. *The Oxford History of the Classical World* (Oxford University Press, 1992).

Bonfante, G. and L., *The Etruscan Language, an Introduction* (Manchester University Press, 2002).

Bowman, Alan K., *Life and Letters on the Roman Frontier, Vindolanda and its People* (The British Museum Press, 1994).

Brown, Michelle P., *A Guide To Western Historical Scripts* (The British Library, 1990).

Crystal, David, *The Cambridge Encyclopedia of the English Language* (Cambridge University Press, 1995).

Crystal, David, *The Cambridge Encyclopedia of Language* (Cambridge University Press, 1997).

Davies, Martin, *Aldus Manutius, Printer and Publisher of Renaissance Venice* (The British Library, 1995).

De Hamel, Christopher, *A History of Illuminated Manuscripts* (Phaidon, 1994).

Fischer, Steven Roger, *A History of Writing* (Reaktion Books, 2003).

Gardiner, Sir Alan, *The Egyptians* (Folio Society, 1999) previously published as *Egypt of the Pharaohs: an Introduction* (Clarendon Press, 1961).

Gray, Nicolete, *A History of Lettering* (Phaidon, 1986).

Harris, David, *The Art of Calligraphy* (Dorling Kindersley, 1995).

Isserlin, B. S. J., 'The Earliest Alphabetic Writing' in *The Cambridge Ancient History, Volume 3, Part 1, The Prehistory of the Balkans: the Middle East, and the Aegean World, Tenth to Eighth Centuries B.C.*, 2nd edition (1982), ed. John Boardman *et al.* (Cambridge University Press, 2003).

Jackson, Donald, *The Story of Writing* (Studio Vista in association with The Parker Pen Company, 1981).

Jeffrey, L. H., 'Greek Alphabetic Writing' in *The Cambridge Ancient History, Volume 3, Part 1, The Prehistory of the Balkans: the Middle East, and the Aegean World, Tenth to Eighth Centuries B.C.*, 2nd edition (1982), ed. John Boardman *et al.* (Cambridge University Press, 2003).

Johnston, Edward, *Writing, Illuminating and Lettering*, revised edition (1939) (Isaac Pitman and Sons, 1946).

Jones, Peter and Sidwell, Keith, *The World of Rome* (Cambridge University Press, 1997).

Markoe, Glenn E., *Phoenicians* (The British Museum Press, 2002).

Mosley, James, 'Trajan Revived' in *Alphabet 1964, Volume 1* (James Moran Ltd for the Kynoch Press, 1964).

Naveh, Joseph, *Origins of the Alphabets* (The Jerusalem Publishing House Ltd).

Potter, T. W., *Roman Italy* (The British Museum Press, 1987).

Reade, Julian, *Mesopotamia* (The British Museum Press, 2000).

Roaf, Michael, *Cultural Atlas of Mesopotamia and the Ancient Near East* (Equinox Books, 1990).

Robinson, Andrew, *The Story of Writing* (Thames and Hudson, 1995).

Sacks, David, *Alphabet: Unravelling the Mystery of the Alphabet from A to Z* (Hutchinson, 2003).

Saggs, H. W. F., *The Babylonians* (Folio Society, 1999), previously published as *The Greatness that was Babylon* (Sidgwick and Jackson, 1988).

Steinberg, S. H., *Five Hundred Years of Printing*, revised by John Trevitt (The British Library and Oak Knoll Press, 1996).

Thorpe, Lewis (trans.), *Two Lives of Charlemagne* (Penguin, 1988).

Van De Mieroop, Marc, *A History of the Ancient Near East, c. 3000–323 BC* (Blackwell Publishing, 2004).

Wilson, Penelope, *Hieroglyphs: A Very Short Introduction* (Oxford University Press, 2004).

Wood, Michael, *Domesday: A Search for the Roots of England* (BBC Books, 1986).

Wood, Michael, *In Search of the Dark Ages* (BBC Books, 1987).

Acknowledgements

The publishers would like to thank Andrew Robinson for his permission to reproduce a version of the clay tablet transcription from his book *The Story of Writing*, reproduced here on page 17.

In addition, the author wishes to express his sincerest thanks to Steven Roger Fischer for his patient, expert advice; Peter Halliday for all his suggestions; Pauline Graham for her naughtiness; Dave, Sarah and Andy for getting me out of a tight postal spot; Tim, Julian and Graham for thinking this was a good idea; and Dara for everything else.

FOR THE FOLIO EDITION
Although this Folio edition of *A is for Ox* still carries its original dedication, I would also like it to be dedicated to Joe Tanner, who died earlier this year: printer, type connoisseur and thoroughly decent chap.

Index

Figures in *italics* refer to illustrations

Valeas qui legis